# Call To Holy Life

## Anthony Lyle

## Gotham Books

30 N Gould St.
Ste. 20820, Sheridan, WY 82801
https://gothambooksinc.com/

Phone: 1 (307) 464-7800

© 2025 *Anthony Lyle*. All rights reserved.

No part of this book may be reproduced, stored in a retrieval system, or transmitted by any means without the written permission of the author.

Published by Gotham Books (April 2, 2025)

ISBN: 979-8-3492-4080-5 (P)
ISBN: 979-8-3492-4081-2 (E)

Because of the dynamic nature of the Internet, any web addresses or links contained in this book may have changed since publication and may no longer be valid.

The views expressed in this work are solely those of the author and do not necessarily reflect the views of the publisher, and the publisher hereby disclaims any responsibility for them.

# Table of Contents

**CHAPTER 1** .................................................................................................. 1
    CALL OF GOD ............................................................................................. 1

**CHAPTER 2** .................................................................................................. 5
    DOES SATAN WANT YOU TO LISTEN TO GOD? ........................................ 5

**CHAPTER 3** .................................................................................................. 7
    FOUNDATIONS OF BELIEF; OBEDIENCE ..................................................... 7

**CHAPTER 4** ................................................................................................ 10
    FOUNDATIONS OF BELIEF FAITH ............................................................ 10

**CHAPTER 5** ................................................................................................ 12
    FOUNDATIONS OF BELIEF: BAPTISMS AND LAYING ON OF HANDS ...... 12

**CHAPTER 6** ................................................................................................ 15
    FOUNDATIONS OF BELIEF RESURRECTION ............................................ 15

**CHAPTER 7** ................................................................................................ 20
    FOUNDATIONS: ETERNAL JUDGEMENT .................................................. 20

**CHAPTER 8** ................................................................................................ 22
    YOUR DUTY TO GOD ............................................................................... 22

**CHAPTER 9** ................................................................................................ 25
    WORD OF GOD ....................................................................................... 25

**CHAPTER 10** .............................................................................................. 29
    EUCHARIST: LORD'S SUPPER .................................................................. 29

**CHAPTER 11** .............................................................................................. 32
    WRATH OF GOD ..................................................................................... 32

**CHAPTER 12** .............................................................................................. 42
    SCROLL OF REVELATION ........................................................................ 42

**CHAPTER 13** .............................................................................................. 51
    THE RAPTURE ........................................................................................ 51

**CHAPTER 14** ............................................................................................. 55
TRIBULATION INTERPRETATION AND OPENING OF THE SEALS .................................... 55
**CHAPTER 15** ............................................................................................. 61
   OPENING THE SEALS ................................................................................. 61
**CHAPTER 16** ........................................................................................... 132
   SUMMARY ............................................................................................ 132
**CHAPTER 17** ........................................................................................... 134
   ABBREVIATIONS ................................................................................... 134

# Chapter 1

## Call of God

Have you ever wondered about how Abraham became so great in the area of serving God? What about Noah? Noah spent 120 years in building an ark on the promise of a small voice inside of him to "build an ark". And Moses was 80 years old when he stopped to see this amazing thing, a burning bush that didn't burn up!

These are some of the more famous "servants of God". And amazingly, while there is sufficient evidence of the existence of Israel, modern scholars are trying to erase these famous people from history. Why? One reason is that they serve God. Anti-God movements are popping up everywhere and not just the U.S.

If you're reading this you have already felt the tug of a living supreme God, or have already answered the "call of God". Do you go to church? Do you get out a Bible and start to read? This book is about fulfilling the call to a devout life of service to the one true living God.

Abraham had no Bible to answer his questions. Noah had no Bible to guide him about building an ark and yet... they accomplished amazing things in the Name of God.

I've seen this time and time again as a person goes up in front of a church and wants to be a better Christian. What do most pastors and leaders do? They make a big show out of it, putting their hands on your shoulder and announcing to the congregation about how you're doing a great thing but....

But they are using your actions to promote their own greatness! And inside you feel it... but don't know what to do about it. They push you into becoming a Sunday school teacher, or the head of a group. Yes, serve "their" interests is the way to serve God is "their answer'.

Noah had no one to tell the world about his great answer to the living God. Noah wasn't even counted as a great man (except by God Himself) until ... well, until Abraham. Abraham lived in the city of Ur when he first heard the "still small voice" of God telling him to leave the city of fire (Ur) at the age of 70. Noah was 480 when he heard the voice tell him to build an ark.

Why did they do it? What if that "voice" wasn't God? If you've tried to tell anyone about possibly hearing that same small voice inside of you, then you've heard the accusations, and many of them were by "Christians".

"You need to be careful...brother or sister... Satan loves to deceive us.... You could be just hearing your own voice inside of you... blah blah blah..."

At the beginning of Yeshua's ministry Jesus answered Satan. The first thing He did was to remove the fetters of the Law from us. Satan asked Him to prove He was the Son of God by changing stones to bread. Yeshua responded: "Man does not live by bread alone... BUT. (Pay attention here as at this moment, Yeshua is no longer speaking to Satan but to you and me) ... by every word that proceeds from the mouth of God."

Huh? Say what? Yeshua wasn't talking about listening to a preacher, or even reading a Bible... but by "every word that proceeds from the Mouth of God."

"Okay... okay, I'm being punked ... Right?"

NO! You're not being pranked. This was what Yeshua (Jesus) said. So how do we know what is coming from the "mouth of God"? Like Noah, Like Abraham, like Elijah, like Moses, you hear it in a still small voice inside of you. They did it... and so can YOU!

NAHHH... what if that's just me thinking to myself...or worse, some demonic trickery?

This author struggled with these questions for months when I first started to listen to every word that came from the mouth of God. God does NOT trick you. God does not lie to you. God does not lead you astray.

Sit down and ask God outright... outright.... If YOU can hear Him, for him to let you know and then... Shut up... and listen. The FIRST words you hear WILL BE GOD. God wants you to listen to Him, and He will not deceive you. I don't care how ridiculous the words you hear may sound, the FIRST words will be God's.

So, you go to your Christian friend or a pastor or ...someone and tell them that you think you heard God. "Are you SURE? Are you sure it was God?"

The first words from the Serpents mouth to Eve were "Did God really say...."

Yeah, your Christian friend is not your friend at this moment. It's not that they're evil but at the moment they ask if "are you sure?" They have become the mouthpiece of the Serpent in the Garden of Eden. The pastor or church leader, he wants you to listen to HIM, not God because he has experience... right? God might just tell you to leave his church and take your money with you.

Elijah wasn't sure so he went into the cave to "Hear God." A storm came, but God was not in it. An earthquake hit, but God wasn't in it. Then Elijah heard the "still small voice" inside of him... and THAT was God!

God found YOU! He's giving you a command or telling you something. In my case, God knew I was worried about who I was listening to, so He gave me a little help and it didn't include any angelic visits. It was just a few things that were going to happen that I could not possibly know on my own. One thing led to another and now some 40 years later, I can't "UNHEAR God". He has become a part of me... and I a part of Him. Simple things too. I walk down the aisle of a grocery store and reach for an item and I hear "no". A soft but firm no. Having experience, I've learned to listen. I've learned to obey. So, I move on. Why didn't God want me to get that item? I have NO idea most of the time. Hashem does not seem too quick to explain Himself to me, but I've learned that He knows best.

"Well, yeah, but there are a lot of crazy people out there who believe they can talk to God."

"Really... are they crazy or is that just the label assigned to them by some NON-BELIEVING psychologist who (drum roll) ...

wants you to believe in THEM... not God. And unfortunately, there are many "Christian leaders" who want that same power over you.

# Chapter 2

## Does Satan want you to listen to God?

First of all, from here on, God will be referred to by a more "respectful" term: HaShem which in Hebrew means "The Name". His name is holy and to use it "in vain" is a problem. HaShem refers to God without directly using His NAME.

King James (Matthew 4) "{4:1} then was Jesus led up of the Spirit into the wilderness to be tempted of the devil. {4:2} and when he had fasted forty days and forty nights, he was afterward an hungred. {4:3} and when the tempter came to him, he said, If thou be the Son of God, command that these stones be made bread. {4:4} But he answered and said, It is written, Man shall not live by bread alone, but by every word that proceeds out of the mouth of God. {4:5} then the devil taketh him up into the holy city, and sets him on a pinnacle of the temple, {4:6} and says unto him, If thou be the Son of God, cast thyself down: for it is written, He shall give his angels charge concerning thee: and in [their] hands they shall bear thee up, lest at any time thou dash thy foot against a stone. {4:7} Jesus said unto him, it is written again, thou shalt not tempt the Lord thy God. {4:8} Again, the devil taketh him up into an exceeding high mountain, and shews him all the kingdoms of the world, and the glory of them; {4:9} And says unto him, All these things will I give thee, if thou wilt fall down and worship me. {4:10} then says Jesus unto him, get thee hence, Satan: for it is written, thou shalt worship the Lord thy God, and him only shalt thou serve."

1. If you are the Son of God...

    a. Satan will question if you really can "hear God!" Ridiculous. All the psychologists say so. Even other Christians don't believe that!

2. Sets Him on the pinnacle of the temple... cast thyself down

    b. Okay, so if you can hear God, say something that God told you. Test God.

3. Takes him to the mountain and shows Yeshua the kingdoms of the world.

    a. Do you believe you now have any power? Don't let this power to hear God tempt you into believing you are sinless and don't need the Salvation of the Blood of Christ. If anything, you should better understand your need for guidance from HaShem. Notice I didn't say guidance from some church leader. I said "from HaShem."

The temptations of Satan will be temptations for you. Once you made the choice to "serve HaShem", the world became your enemy. If you do find someone to believe you, in you, then HaShem has blessed you. You will experience many "friends and relatives" who while appearing to be on your side will disappear from your circle.

# Chapter 3

# Foundations of Belief: Obedience

The Book of Hebrews chapter 6 verses 1 to 6 actually gives you the first principals of belief for the new Christian. These instructions are the "milk of the word". The understanding of these principals cannot come before your answer to the Call of God. They come AFTER you have answered that call. You have become a Messianic Believer, a Believer in the Risen Christ. So, you're ready to begin your walk with Hashem.

There are 6 subjects listed. There is a seventh subject but that will be revealed later. It is not found in this list.

The first item: *Repentance from Dead Works*: It does not read "Repentance from sin." You did that already when you acknowledged Christ on the Cross for your sins! This is different. This is the only place in the entire Bible where this Greek word (translated into English) is used.

Dead work. What is a dead work? Any work that is not from or permitted by HaShem. Whoa... nothing you do on your own is considered of any value to HaShem. Seriously? Nothing?

You have chosen to answer to the living God and He will instruct your ways. He will guide your path of righteousness.

This subject is about "obedience". It is followed by the next subject, Faith. Why in that order? Because obedience leads to a greater faith in HaShem. Disobedience leads to a lack of faith, to fear, to confusion. This is how you know when you've gotten on the wrong track. You feel confused and unsure.

When you are obedient to HaShem, confusion disappears. You will feel the confidence of a correct choice.

What is the difference between a dead work and a sin? A sin is any action or thought against the Laws of Moses.

Let's say that you come to a corner and you're going to cross the street. No sin in that that can be seen in the Laws of Moses. BUT if you hear the voice of HaShem tell you not to cross the street, and you do it anyway, THAT is a dead work. It has no value to HaShem.

Repentance from Dead Works is about obedience to HaShem. This is a minute by minute obedience

A dead work does not reproduce in fruit but obedience bears fruit.

Repentance is not about "Saying you're sorry." There is nothing in the Word of God that says if you say you're sorry than whatever you said or did is NOT stricken from the Books of God. "I'm sorry" has NO meaning before HaShem. "I'm Sorry" is a human response to other humans ONLY.

How do you repent?

- (King James, Book of James) "Wherefore he says, God resists the proud, but giveth grace unto the humble. {4:7} *submit yourselves therefore to God.* Resist the devil, and he will flee from you... {4:10} humble yourselves in the sight of the Lord, and he shall lift you up."

HUMBLE yourselves. It does not say for HaShem to humble you, but for you to "choose to be humble before HaShem. Resist Pride". This is a choice that you make, not God although He might cause you to be humbled if you refuse.

{4:15} for that ye [ought] to say, If the Lord will, we shall live, and do this, or that. {4:16} but now ye rejoice in your boastings: all such rejoicing is evil. {4:17} Therefore to him that knows to do good, and doeth [it] not, to him it is sin.

- Repentance is a change of direction of choices. Choose a new direction, the one that Hashem has given you to follow.
- {3:18} and the fruit of righteousness is sown in peace of them that make peace.
- A correct choice will bring peace.
- Resist the devil, and he will flee from you.

- The devil is usually behind every bad decision, so resist him. As believers in Christ, you have the power in the NAME OF CHRIST to resist the devil.

# Chapter 4

# Foundations of Belief Faith

(King James- Book of Hebrews) "{6:1} Therefore leaving the principles of the doctrine of Christ, let us go on unto perfection; not laying again the foundation of repentance from dead works, *and of faith toward God,*" The MT says move ahead to maturity.

Obedience is followed by faith, both literally AND Spiritually. This faith is not the same as the "Gift of Faith found in Corinthians". This is a maturing faith that grows the more we are obedient to HaShem. It grows stronger with each obedient act.

The faith in the Gifts of the Spirit is supernatural in that people who have this gift just naturally are able to receive miracle for themselves through this faith. Not so, this maturing faith of obedience. They both have the same term,

James: Emunah ("reliance, assurance", STRG4102). This is the same word used in I Corinthians 12 for the gift of faith, but in Corinthians it is a "gift of faith". It doesn't come with maturity through obedience.

This becomes the path to righteousness, a new life guided by Hashem. It changes you over time. Trials and tribulations will be set before you and each one intended to help you grow "in faith".

It may seem that this is a new enslavement, to God, but in reality, it is a new freedom. Hashem knows everything that is good for your growth, every right decision. Worrying will take a back seat to this faith if you allow it. The problems that come will more than likely be problems that you create as you try to continue with plans that you had for yourself. God has a plan for you.

We are taught to seek "greatness" in life. The best singer, to be great in the "eyes of the world". Awards, riches, success, and power. If you look at truly successful people in the world they are not servants of the most High God. They serve themselves.

This author is not famous. This author is not rich in money or things. I was "arrested by HaShem from becoming a smashing success". I can tell you there is no better life than the simple humble life of obedience to HaShem. In return for financial and "success", HaShem has rewarded me with a greater richness by giving me understanding. Each time I read the Word of God, He shows me something new and it's exciting!

Sure, I still have troubles, but HaShem takes care of them and I have no anxiety or day to day fear about what's going to happen to me. The one sure thing that I rely on is that I serve a stable God who never changes and I never have to worry about if the rules are going to change on me. He is the same as He was yesterday, and today, and tomorrow. "Eyeh asher Eyeh". His name given to Moses "I am what I am" or "I will be what I will be."

# Chapter 5

# Foundations of Belief: Baptisms and Laying on of Hands

This is the only time that the word "baptisms" (plural form) is used in the entire Word of God. It refers to more than one baptism: Baptism in water and baptism in fire. The baptism in water is pretty well understood.

The only debate in this baptism is either sprinkling or dunking. This baptism is NOT required for salvation. The thief on the cross next to Yeshua was not baptized, but he still saw Paradise. Many churches believe this sacrament is required for salvation.

Roman Catholics are so adamant about this sacrament that they believe in child baptism after the child is born. They believe that if a child is not baptized before he dies, he does not go to heaven. The truth is according to Paul is that a child is automatically regarded by HaShem according to the faith of the parent. If just one parent is considered a child of HaShem, then the child is as well.

The big debate about baptism by water is whether it requires complete dunking or is sprinkling okay?

(King James-Matthew) "{3:16} and Jesus, when he was baptized, went up straightway out of the water: and, lo, the heavens were opened unto him, and he saw the Spirit of God descending like a dove, and lighting upon him:"

Yeshua "came up out of the water", meaning that Yeshua went under the water for His baptism by John. There is a non-canon book called the Didache (Didakay), which tells instructions concerning many doctrines for new or young Christians.

(Didache-chapter 7): "7 Concerning Baptism

7:1 Concerning baptism, you should baptize this way: After first explaining all things, baptize in the name

of the Father, and of the Son, and of the Holy Spirit, in flowing water.

7:2 But if you have no running water, baptize in other water; and if you cannot do so in cold water, then in warm.

7:3 If you have very little, pour water three times on the head in the name of Father and Son and Holy Spirit.

7:4 Before the baptism, both the baptizer and the candidate for baptism, plus any others who can,

should fast. The candidate should fast for one or two days beforehand."

It would appear that according to the Apostles the method depends on the available resources.

Baptism by fire is the second form of baptism, "Receiving the Holy Spirit". Acts 2 talks about the first public baptism upon the Apostles, after Christ died and rose again. This baptism took place after the 40 days that Yeshua had returned from the dead.

The Holy Spirit "fell upon the disciples". They didn't have to ask for it. They didn't have to dance in a circle round a fire chanting. They didn't even understand it, until it happened. When it happened, they began to speak in other languages.

Pentecostal and Charismatic Churches put a lot of weight on "being able to speak in tongues" but they are not referring to earthly languages. If you don't get "your tongues" you don't have the Holy Spirit and in many churches like this you might not be "saved".

The important thing is that this baptism comes from HaShem. You don't have to "ask for it" if you are giving your life to God. It might come with some form of outward exhibit, and it might not. You can't buy it (as the false wizard tried to do from Peter). It is NOT in your control.

I Corinthians 12 talks about the "Gifts of the Spirit" but many readers will miss the fact that this chapter also contains a "test" of the true believer. "A true believer will be able to confess that Yeshua came in the flesh and rose again." Amazingly, if one is not a true believer in Yeshua, you will NOT be able to make this confession. Demons are not allowed to confess that Yeshua is the Lord of all. A false believer, if challenged, will somehow avoid making the confession.

In Acts, some did receive the Baptism of the Holy Spirit by the "Laying on of hands". This is when members of the true church lay their hands on someone and pray for him. This isn't just for the Baptism of the Holy Spirit but also for healing and miracles.

# Chapter 6

# Foundations of Belief Resurrection

The term Resurrection is often confused with "raising of the dead". They are not the same. Lazarus was raised from the dead but this was not his final resurrection. Christ on the other hand was also raised from the dead *and* this was His resurrection as He went on from the terrestrial to the Spiritual heavenly to sit at the right hand of God. Therefore, He is the "firstborn" of the resurrection.

Likewise, the word "rapture" is a modern theologian invention. This word does not exist in the entire Word of God. It does refer to the Resurrection in the Last Days, just after Lucifer is cast out of heaven.

When Yeshua came out of the grave, He says something interesting to the women: "Do not touch me as I have not yet gone up to the father." After being on earth for 40 days, He then goes back up to the Father to sit at the right hand of God.

His resurrection was the first resurrection of the "sleeping dead". When Samuel appeared before Saul because of the Witch of Endor, he says to Saul..." Why have you awakened me from my sleep?"

Samuel was dead to this world, but he considered himself to be asleep. He came from Sheol which is not the equivalent of Hell. It was the land of the dead. It was where all the Old Testament Patriarchs were sleeping in death to wait for the "Resurrection."

(King James-Esdra) "{2:23} Wheresoever thou find the dead, take them and bury them, and I will give thee the first place in my resurrection. {2:24} abide still, O my people, and *take thy rest*, for thy quietness still come.

When Yeshua rose to the father the first time He couldn't be touched because he was still going to see the Father. When He was crucified, He had the "keys to Sheol". Daniel' depiction of Christ at the time of Daniel does not describe Yeshua having any keys. Revelation of John however, does describe Yeshua with keys. Where did He get the keys? He got the keys when he died on the Cross and went down to "Sheol" to free the souls that "believed on the Messiah".

(King James-Matthew) "{27:50} Jesus, when he had cried again with a loud voice, yielded up the ghost. {27:51} And, behold, the veil of the temple was rent in twain from the top to the bottom; and the earth did quake, and the rocks rent; {27:52} And the *graves were opened; and many bodies of the saints which slept arose,* {27:53} And came out of the graves after his resurrection, and went into the holy city, and appeared unto many."

(King James- I Peter) "{3:21} The like figure whereunto [even] baptism doth also now save us (not the putting away of the filth of the flesh, but the answer of a good conscience toward God,) by the resurrection of Jesus Christ: {3:22} Who is gone into heaven, and is on the right hand of God; angels and authorities and powers being made subject unto him."

Backtrack a little: Abraham was not a Jew. He was not an Israelite (descendent of Jacob). The covenant of Abraham uses the words "His seed" twice in the promise of Abraham's seed. The first time the word seed referred to Isaac. The second use of the word seed (in the same promise) referred to the Messiah, the descendant of Abraham to rule "forever". Abraham started a new people- Messianic Believer. Abraham understood that the covenant promise of God was telling him about the coming Messiah. Abraham's descendants became "Messianic Believers" before they became Israelites or Jews.

(King James-Matthew) "{22:31} But as touching the resurrection of the dead, have ye not read that which was spoken unto you by God, saying, {22:32} I am the God of Abraham, and the God of Isaac, and the God of Jacob? God is not the God of the dead, but of the living."

These descendants went to a place to sleep upon their death to wait for the Messiah. Yeshua had the keys to Sheol and when He died and went to Sheol, DEATH could not hold Him. He rose again taking with him, all the patriarchs in Sheol to heaven and this is why He had to go to the Father first after rising from the deed to deliver the "Witnesses" who would attend the Wedding of Christ in the End of Days.

These Old Testament Saints were members of the first resurrection lead by Christ. Christ then went to heaven after spending 40 days no earth to take His place and start being our Kohen Gadol, our Holy Priest. He was not yet make King of Kings. That takes place just after Satan or Lucifer is cast out of heaven in the Tribulation. When Lucifer is cast out of heaven, Christ redeems the world from Satan's grasp and becomes King of Kings for 1000 years.

Talking to the saints and apostles: (Mark)" {14:12} Then said he also to him that bade him, When thou make a dinner or a supper, call not thy friends, nor thy brethren, neither thy kinsmen, nor [thy] rich neighbors; lest they also bid thee again, and a recompense be made thee. {14:13} But when thou make a feast, call the poor, the maimed, the lame, the blind: {14:14} and thou shalt be blessed; for they cannot recompense thee: for thou shalt be recompensed at the *resurrection of the just.*

(King James-John) "{5:21} for as the Father raises up the dead, and quickens [them;] even so the Son quickens whom he will." ... The hour is coming, and now is, when the dead shall hear the voice of the Son of God: and they that hear shall live. {5:26} for as the Father hath life in himself; so hath he given to the Son to have life in himself; {5:27} and hath given him authority to execute judgment also, because he is the Son of man. {5:28} Marvel not at this: for the hour is coming, in the which all that are in the graves shall hear his voice, {5:29} And shall come forth; they that have done good, unto the resurrection of life; and they that have done evil, unto the resurrection of damnation... {11:23} Jesus says unto her, Thy brother shall rise again. {11:24} Martha says unto him, I know that he shall rise again in the resurrection at the last day. {11:25} Jesus said unto her, I am the resurrection, and the life: he that believes in me, though he were dead, yet shall he live: {11:26} and whosoever lives and believeth in me shall never die. Believe thou this?

(King James- I Corinthians) "{15:21} for since by man [came] death, by man [came] also the resurrection of the dead. {15:22} for as in Adam all die, even so in Christ shall all be made alive.... {15:35} But some [man] will say, how are the dead raised up? And with what body do they come? {15:36} [Thou] fool, that which thou sow is not quickened, except it die: {15:37} And that which thou sow, thou sow not that body that shall be, but bare grain, it may chance of wheat, or of some other [grain] 15:38} But God giveth it a body as it hath pleased him, and to every seed his own body. {15:39} All flesh [is] not the same flesh: but [there is] one [kind of] flesh of men, another flesh of beasts, another of fishes, [and] another of birds. {15:40} [There are] also celestial bodies, and bodies terrestrial: but the glory of the celestial [is] one, and the [glory] of the terrestrial [is] another. {15:41} [There is] one glory of the sun, and another glory of the moon, and another glory of the stars: for [one] star differs from [another] star in glory. {15:42} so also [is] the resurrection of the dead. It is sown in corruption; it is raised in incorruption: {15:43} It is sown in dishonor; it is raised in glory: it is sown in weakness; it is raised in power: {15:44} It is sown a natural body; it is raised a spiritual body. There is a natural body, and there is a spiritual body. {15:45} and so it is written, the first man Adam was made a living soul; the last Adam [was made] a quickening spirit. {15:46} Howbeit that [was] not first which is spiritual, but that which is natural; and afterward that which is spiritual. {15:47} the first man [is] of the earth, earthy: the second man [is] the Lord from heaven. {15:48} as [is] the earthy, such [are] they also that are earthy: and as [is] the heavenly, such [are] they also that are heavenly. {15:49} And as we have borne the image of the earthy, we shall also bear the image of the heavenly... {15:51} Behold, I shew you a mystery; we shall not all sleep, but we shall all be changed, {15:52} in a moment, in the twinkling of an eye, at the last trump: for the trumpet shall sound, and the dead shall be raised incorruptible, and we shall be changed. {15:53} for this corruptible must put on incorruption, and this mortal [must] put on immortality."

He appoints an angel and gives that angel a sickle to "harvest" everyone with the "Name of God." This becomes the resurrection or what we refer to now as "Rapture" of the Saints of Post-Crucifix Messianic Believers.

The wicked dead remain in Sheol asleep waiting for the final Resurrection of the Wicked Dead, at the Great White Throne of God. This is the third resurrection but it only contains the wicked dead, those who rejected Christ and God throughout their life.

The righteous who are resurrected wait here for the Wedding of Yeshua and his Bride, along with the Old Testament Witnesses to the wedding.

Sheol is not hell. There is no hell in existence except in movies. The place that is actually hell is the "Lake of the Fire".

(King James - Revelation) "{20:1} and I saw an angel come down from heaven, having the key of the bottomless pit and a great chain in his hand. {20:2} And he laid hold on the dragon, that old serpent, which is the Devil, and Satan, and bound him a thousand years, {20:3} And cast him into the bottomless pit, and shut him up, and set a seal upon him, that he should deceive the nations no more, till the thousand years should be fulfilled: and after that he must be loosed a little season. {20:4} And I saw thrones, and they sat upon them, and judgment was given unto them: and [I saw] the souls of them that were beheaded for the witness of Jesus, and for the word of God, and which had not worshipped the beast, neither his image, neither had received [his] mark upon their foreheads, or in their hands; and they lived and reigned with Christ a thousand years. {20:5} But the rest of the dead lived not again until the thousand years were finished. This [is] the first resurrection. {20:6} blessed and holy [is] he that hath part in the first resurrection: on such the second death hath no power, but they shall be priests of God and of Christ, and shall reign with him a thousand years. {20:7} and when the thousand years are expired, Satan shall be loosed out of his prison,"

# Chapter 7

# Foundations: Eternal Judgement

One way or another we will all be judged by our Savior or Hashem. The righteous who chose to believe on Him who was crucified and rose again will be judged by our Lord and Savior. The wicked will be judged at the Great White Throne at the end of time by Hashem the Omega.

Judgement comes in two flavors; Righteous or made clean by the Blood of Christ or wicked. The wicked will be sent to the Lake of the Fire. This as close to a definition of Hell as ever made in the Word of God: The Lake of the fire is exactly that, a lake of pure fire, but this is no ordinary fire.

It will burn the souls of all who are sent there without consuming those souls. This is the same as the Burning Bush of Moses. The fire burned but did not consume.

More than that, it will give no light. No photons will come out of this fire. Darkness will not be passive as our darkness is on earth (subject to lack of light), but will be proactively destroying light.

The laws of the Lake of the Fire do not follow the Laws of Physics. Heaven and earth are destroyed at the final judgement due to the fact that they are witnesses to our sins and that will not be allowed to those who are judged as righteous due to our obedience to HaShem. A NEW heaven and earth will be created with HaShem as the source of all light. Any judgement passed by either court, the court of Yeshua or the court of the Great White Throne of God, is permanent and forever. There will be no Court of Appeals. No one will be able to bribe the final Judge. His judgement will be everlasting and just.

For the wicked, this is scary. For the believers who maintained their faith in Yeshua HaMaschiach this is a relief. There will be no prosecuting or defense lawyers to make private deals behind the scenes. Our "accuser", HaSatan, will be defeated once and for all and he too will be sent to the Lake of the Fire and won't even be allowed in the courtroom of God.

# Chapter 8

## Your Duty to God

King James (Exodus) "{27:30} and all the tithe of the land, [whether] of the seed of the land, [or] of the fruit of the tree, [is] the LORD'S: [it is] holy unto the LORD. {27:31} and if a man will at all redeem [ought] of his tithes, he shall add thereto the fifth [part] thereof. {27:32} and concerning the tithe of the herd, or of the flock, [even] of whatsoever passes under the rod, the tenth shall be holy unto the LORD."

What's wrong with this? Nothing. It was written by Moses around 1500 BC. But this is superseded by the new command of Yeshua. "…but… by every word that proceeds from the mouth of God…"

Yes, Yeshua gave us a new law after He came and "fulfilled" the Law of Moses. One rule that allows us to live our life in righteousness. This was the first thing that Yeshua did when he finished the 40-day temptation was to give us this command in response to Satan's temptation. First Thing before He started his ministry in Galilee. First thing before He gave the famous message of Isaiah. This should be our first thing too… to learn to listen to every word that proceeds from the mouth of HaShem!!!

But… but… but… aren't we supposed to support our churches and pastors? Sure, *if that's what HaShem wants you to do.* Whoa did I just say that? I don't know how many times, I have asked Hashem if I should give money to a ministry and He said "NO!" But I have given untold amounts of money to poor individuals and families who really needed the money.

I was at a church one time when a poorly dressed beggar came into the church and I just happened to be talking to the Pastor there. The man asked for some money to eat. The Pastor refused. I could tell the Pastor was embarrassed, but then he explained himself. "Well, he'll just use it to buy liquor or drugs."

HUH?  So, what?  How the beggar spends the money is between the beggar and HaShem. There is nothing ...NOTHING in the Bible that dictates that WE are to pass judgement on the needy. Now if HaShem told that pastor not to give the beggar money, that's another situation, but the pastor didn't ASK GOD! He made the decision on his own.

I listened to one pastor for 6 months on their show and out of that there were no less than 7 messages about our "duty to giving". But in those messages was not ONE message about asking HaShem about doing what HaShem wants. The messages were about doing what the *messenger* wanted not what HaShem wanted.

And it goes deeper. When HaShem commands you to give money to anyone, or any organization, only give the exact amount. Giving 1 penny more so you can earn a gold star is not obedience. It is DISOBEDIENCE.

At the beginning of Moses in Exodus, they came to the Waters of Mariah. Moses was told to strike the rocks and low and behold water gushed from the rocks. Enough to slake the thirst of 2 million people AND their animals.

In the last year of the wandering, year 40, they came back to the waters of Mariah and Hashem tells Moses to wave his staff over the rocks. (Pause here to see if you got that). WAVE his staff. Moses *strikes the rocks* just like he did at the beginning of the 40 years.

As a result of his disobedience (HaShem told him to only WAVE his staff), Moses was allowed to "see the promised land" from a nearby mountain but he was not allowed to enter the land. God expects "EXACT" obedience, not what you THINK He wants.

If He tells you to give 20 dollars to a beggar (even if that beggar might buy drugs), He expects that you will give EXACTLY 20 dollars, not 20.01... not 19.99. EXACTLY 20.00. I know. I know. Sound extreme, don't I?  But HaShem doesn't expect us to "Guess what He wants us to so".

Going to church is another issue. Did HaShem tell you to go to church? Did HaShem tell you to go to THAT church? Hm. so what I'm saying is that obedience to God requires minute by minute obedience. Yep, that's it.

I know, it's HARD to do at first, but now after 40 years of doing this, this author doesn't know how to live any other way. Even this book was on His command to me. I don't make much money off of my books. I deliberately choose to take little to no royalties for any of my books as I don't want to be guilty before HaShem for trying to "sell HIS work as my own."

# Chapter 9

# Word of God

This author does not read or understand Hebrew, Greek, Arabic, or any other language of the original versions of the Bible. Like most of you, I am reliant on trustworthy translators to translate a version of the Bible into English.

There are three Greek texts of the New Testament available to translators, called the Majority Text (MT), Textus Receptus (TR), and Critical Text (CT). A translation uses one of these.

3. **M - Majority Text (MT).** The translation's New Testament is based on the Majority Text, which represents an approximate (or weighted) majority of all available manuscripts for each verse.
4. **T - Textus Receptus (TR).** The translation's New Testament is based on the Textus Receptus, which is what the King James Version (KJV) used. The TR is a majority text based on manuscripts available in the 1500s. Except for Revelation, it's very close to today's Majority Text. If a translation has neither M-trait nor T-trait, then it's based on the Critical Text (CT), which was first assembled in the 1800s and is the basis of most modern translations.

A translation is said to be "literal" if it translates every Greek or Hebrew word into English, usually keeping the same tense, with little regard for making the English smooth. However, word-order in Greek and Hebrew differs from English, so most literal translations re-order the words for you. They will even interpolate words for you (always in italics). Literal translations are often more wordy because they add words to accurately express tenses. So, although reading literal translations is a slow and bumpy ride, they are not as rough as you would think, and are excellent for careful study. Some popular translations, such as the NKJV, KJV, and NASB, are regarded as literal, but that means they are *mostly* literal; none of them is 100% literal like those with the L-trait.

The version of choice for this author is the 1611 Version of the King James Bible. I avoid all English versions that have been published (and require large costly dollar amounts) after 1957. This includes the New International, the Amplified, the Parallel, The New American Standard, and all new recent versions. Almost all of these newer versions were translated into English from the Wescott and Hort version of Bede's Greek.

Wescott and Hort were Bishops in the Church of England around 1850. What few know is that they were secretly members of the Ghostly Guild, an offshoot of the Illuminati. Their goal was to give a version of the Bible that in many "Many" cases, the words Lord, Jesus, and God were changed to allow the possible interpretation of "Lord Satan, Lucifer, etc." They removed or modified over 64000 words of the original Bede Greek version.

These are a few examples:

1: Luke 9:56 and you will read: "For the Son of Man did not come to destroy men's lives but to save them." And they went to another village.

Now, compare that to NIV:

1. Then he and his disciples went to another village.

2. Matthew 18:11 is completely removed from the NIV.

3. John 5:4 is completely missing from the NIV.

4. Matthew 5:44 is missing a large portion of the original verse.

5. Mark 11:26 is missing from the NIV version.

6. And the WORST of all: Luke 4:4:

The NiV reads: Jesus answered, "It is written: 'Man shall not live on bread alone.'

The original reads: But Jesus answered him, saying, "It is written, 'Man shall not live by bread alone, *but by every word of God.*'"

7. Perversions of the Lord's Prayer can be found in Luke 11:2 and Matthew 6:13 where portions of the verse are missing.

The NIV adds words that aren't intended to be there:

1. Mark 7:19: NIV - For it doesn't go into their heart but into their stomach, and then out of the body." (In saying this, Jesus declared all foods clean.)

KJV - because it does not enter his heart but his stomach, and is eliminated, thus purifying all foods?"

The problem is since Tyndale's English translation in 1526, translators and publishers have created approximately 900 different English Bibles, making it hard to know which to choose. Translating from Hebrew to English or Greek to English can be difficult to say the least.

This author found that the JPS (Jewish Publication Society) translates from the earliest known Hebrew versions to English. But, in the end, how do you know?

For one Hebrew example, notice how a selection of translations will render the Hebrew word *rakhum* (mercy, compassion) in Psalm 79:8.

Psalms 79:8 Do not remember the iniquities of our forefathers against us; Let Your compassion come quickly to meet us, for we are brought very low.

King James Version, KJV O remember not against us former iniquities: let thy tender mercies (Heb. rakhum) speedily prevent us: for we are brought very low.New American Standard Bible, NASB

Do not hold us responsible for the guilty deeds of our forefathers; let your compassion (Heb. *rakhum*) come quickly to meet us, for we have become very low. New International Version, NIV.

Do not hold against us the sins of past generations; may your mercy (Heb. *rakhum*) come quickly to meet us, for we are in desperate need.

New Living Translation, NLT Do not hold us guilty for the sins of our ancestors! Let your compassion (Heb. *rakhum*) quickly meet our needs, for we are on the brink of despair.

Contemporary English Version, CEVDon't make us pay for the sins of our ancestors. Have pity (Heb. *rakhum*) and come quickly! We are completely helpless. *The Message*, MSGDon't blame us for the sins of our parents. Hurry up and help (Heb. *rakhum*) us; we're at the end of our rope.

*The Living Bible*, TLBOh, do not hold us guilty for our former sins! Let your tenderhearted mercies (Heb. *rakhum*) meet our needs, for we are brought low to the dust.

It's clear we have more than one way to understand the Hebrew word *rakhum*: tender mercies, compassion, mercy, pity, help, and tenderhearted mercies. Seeing and respecting variations helps us humbly continue the work it takes to understand the words of others. We can see how multiple English renderings of the same idea give us a deeper understanding of *rakhum*, not to mention all the other words.

This problem is not limited to a translation of the Hebrew, but Galatians 3:24 from different versions of English from the Greek give different interpretations of the word "paidagogos"- guardian, schoolmaster, tutor, teacher, and disciplinarian.

Mark Overton gives his review of the accuracy of different versions: The NKJV and KJV are significantly more accurate than all other popular translations. The NASB, CSB, and ESV are mediocre. The GNT, NLT, and NIV are poor, failing nearly every pressure-verse.

Just ask HaShem to guide you. That's the BEST that you can do. Do what HaShem tells you to do and ask Him to show you the "truth" of His Word.

# Chapter 10

## Eucharist: Lord's Supper

Paul wrote to the Corinthians (King James) "{11:23} for I have received of the Lord that which also I delivered unto you, that the Lord Jesus the [same] night in which he was betrayed took bread:

{11:24} And when he had given thanks, he brake [it,] and said, Take, eat: this is my body, which is broken for you: this do in remembrance of me. {11:25} after the same manner also [he took] the cup, when he had supped, saying, this cup is the New Testament in my blood: this do ye, as oft as ye drink [it,] in remembrance of me. {11:26} for as often as ye eat this bread, and drink [this] cup, ye do shew the

Lord's death till he come. {11:27} wherefore whosoever shall eat this bread, and drink this cup of the Lord, unworthily, shall be guilty of the body and blood of the Lord. {11:28} but let a man examine himself, and so let him eat of [that] bread, and drink of [that] cup. {11:29} for he that eats and drinks unworthily, eats and drinks damnation to himself, not discerning the Lord's body. {11:30} for this cause many [are] weak and sickly among you, and many sleeps. {11:31} for if we would judge ourselves, we should not be judged. {11:32} But when we are judged, we are chastened of the Lord, that we should not be condemned with the world. {11:33} wherefore, my brethren, when ye come together to eat, tarry one for another. {11:34} And if any man hunger, let him eat at home; that ye come not together unto condemnation. And the rest will I set in order when I come."

(Didache of the Apostles) Eucharist "9:1 concerning the Eucharist, give thanks this way.

9:2 first, concerning the cup: We thank you, our Father, for the holy vine of David your servant, which you made known to us through Jesus your servant. To you be the glory forever. 9:3 next, concerning the broken bread: We thank you, our Father, for the life and knowledge which you made known to us through Jesus your servant. To you be the glory forever. 9:4 Even as this broken bread was scattered over the hills, and was gathered together and became one, so let your church be gathered together from the ends of the earth into your kingdom. To you is the glory and the power through Jesus Christ forever. 9:5 allow no one to eat or drink of your Eucharist, unless they have been baptized in the name of the Lord. For concerning this, the Lord has said, "Do not give what is holy to dogs." 10 After the Eucharist 10:1 After the Eucharist when you are filled, give thanks this way: 10:2 We thank you, holy Father, for your holy name which you enshrined in our hearts, and for the knowledge and faith and immortality that you made known to us through Jesus your servant. To you be the glory forever.

10:3 You, Master Almighty, have created all things for your name's sake. You gave food and drink to all people for enjoyment that they might give thanks to you; but to us you freely give spiritual food and drink and life eternal through Jesus, your servant. 10:4 before all things we thank you because you are mighty. To you be the glory forever. 10:5 Remember, Lord, your church. Deliver it from all evil and make it perfect in your love, and gather it from the four winds sanctified for your kingdom which you have prepared for it. For yours is the power and the glory forever. 10:6 let grace come, and let this world pass away! Hosanna to the Son of David! If anyone is holy, let him come; if anyone is not holy, let him repent. Maranatha! Amen."

The Catholic Church teaches that the Eucharist is "Transubstantiated" so that when the Lord's Supper is taken, it is the "actual body of Christ". There is nothing in the the Bible that supports this. It is totally a Roman Catholic belief: Transubstantiation is a theological term derived from two Latin roots, trans (prefix), a preposition that means "over" or "across," and substantia (root), a noun that means "substance." To transubstantiate is to change one substance into another. The initial substance is bread and wine, and it changes into a new and different substance, the Body and Blood of Christ. It is no longer bread, but the Body of Christ under the appearance of bread; and no longer wine, but the Blood of Christ under the appearance of wine.

Historically, transubstantiation was first taught by the Fourth Lateran Council in 1215, and reaffirmed, clarified, and strengthened at the Council of Constance in 1415 and the Council of Trent in 1551.

It is important to note that taking the bread and wine "rightly" is important as if taken in corruption can lead to sickness as pointed out in I Corinthians. One does not need a minister to administer the Lord's Supper. A family can partake of this in private on their own.

Many churches substitute kool-aid for real wine. Their reasoning is that they don't want to tempt "alcoholics". Addiction is another subject and not to be covered here but this author opposes substituting a child's drink for the wine. But you do whatever HaShem tells you to do.

# Chapter 11

## Wrath of God

This section is a bit more advanced in understanding the Belief in Christ Who Is Risen, but new believers find the end of Days complicated. This section is intended to give a basic understanding of the End of Days.

(LXXTR-Romans 1) "Therefore God also gave them up to uncleanness in the lusts of their own hearts, to dishonor their own bodies with each other: 1:25 who exchanged the truth of God for a lie, and worshipped and served the creature more than the Creator, who is blessed forever. Amen. 1:26 For this because God gave them up to dishonorable affections: for both the females among them have quit the natural intimacy for that which is against nature 1:27 And likewise also the males, leaving the natural intimacy with the female, burned in their lust toward one another; males committing with males that which is unfitting, and receiving in themselves that recompense for their error which was due. 1:28 And according as they did not like to retain God in their knowledge, God gave them over to a reprobate mind, to do those things which are not fitting; 1:29 Being filled with all unrighteousness, fornication, wickedness, covetousness, maliciousness; full of envy, murder, debate, deceit, malignity; they are whisperers, 1:30 backbiters, haters of God, despiteful, proud, boasters, inventors of evil things, disobedient to parents, 1:31 Without understanding, covenant breakers, without natural affection, implacable, unmerciful: 1:32 Who knowing the judgment of God, that they which commit such things are worthy of death, not only do the same, but give approval to those that commit them... But after your hardness and impenitent heart you are storing up wrath upon yourself against the *day of wrath* and revelation of the righteous judgment of God; 2:6 Who will render to every person according to his deeds... 3:10 As it is written, there is none righteous, no, not one: 3:11 There is no one that understands, there is no one that seeks after God. 3:12 They are all gone out of the way, they are together become unprofitable; there is no one who does good, no, not one. 3:13 Their throat is an open sepulcher; with their tongues they have used deceit; the poison of asps is under their lips: 3:14 Whose mouth is full of cursing and bitterness: 3:15 Their feet are swift to shed blood: 3:16 Destruction and misery are in their ways: 3:17 And the way of peace they have not known: 3:18 There is no fear of God before their eyes."

(MTJ-Romans) "|26| for this reason, Hashem (in wrath) delivered them over to paskudneh ("contemptible") sexual desires. For their females traded off natural sexual intercourse for unnatural.

|27| Likewise also the males abandoned natural sexual intercourse with the female counterpart and were inflamed with craving for one another, males with males committing what is indecent and receiving back ("in exchange") in themselves the appropriate gemul ("retribution" YESHAYAH 3:11) for their toyus ("error")."

The feminism movement, intended to empower females, has fallen away against the sexual freedom that exists, allowing all sorts of "lusts to their own bodies." Crime and injustice prevail in every nation around the globe. Men and women have become slaves to their corrupt natures.

(LXXTR-II Timothy) "3:1 this know also, that in the last days perilous times shall come. 3:2 For men shall be lovers of their own selves, covetous, boasters, proud, blasphemers, disobedient to parents, unthankful, unholy, 3:3 Without natural affection, trucebreakers, false accusers, incontinent, fierce, despisers of those that are good, 3:4 Traitors, heady, high-minded, lovers of pleasures more than lovers of God; 3:5 Having a form of godliness, but denying the power of it: from such turn away. 3:6 for of this sort are they which creep into houses, and lead captive silly women laden with sins, led away with different lusts, 3:7 Ever learning, and never able to come to the knowledge of the truth."

While churches often boast of their growing numbers, it is ironic that the Bible predicts a *falling away during the last days.* It is amazing that the prophetic messages taking place in the churches (where such messages are allowed) predict revival when the only revival predicted in the Bible is that of the Jewish nation ("the vision of the Dry Bones of Ezekiel").

Even during the Times of the Israelites, descendants of Jacob were responsible to HaShem at an individual level. The rebellions against Moses by his own people should be example enough of this. It was not intended for the Church to rid the world of sin. If this were so, the need for Yeshua to "be crucified" or return to earth at the *end of days* would not be necessary.

The final insult to HaShem, to Christ, is that modern churches brag about how many people they have gotten to the altar for "the altar call", claiming this is victory. The evidence of Abraham through the 3 covenants shows that the "call of HaShem" is only the beginning of the salvation walk with Christ. If those who come to the altar call do not continue with Christ of what benefit was their initial tears of repentance. The message to the churches is further warning that the churches needed to cling to faith in Christ. The last message shows that many members of "the church" are lukewarm and will be spewed out!

The Doctrine of "Once Saved Always Saved" does not have scriptural support. The Book of Hebrews mentions blasphemy against the Holy Spirit as a cause to fall away from following Christ and once this sin has taken place, the person is no longer eligible for a seat at Christ's feast. This is predicted in the type represented by the Pharaoh of Egypt during the Exodus. After he rejected HaShem so many times, *HaShem took away his free will to repent.* This will be true of many in the last days.

Because we are all sons and daughters of Adam our natures are evil from the beginning. The thought that we could "Lose our salvation" because of our sins scared the churches. The doctrine of once saved always saved was created *by the church* to ease those fears, but this same doctrine allows us to give in to our carnal natures thinking we don't have to worry about "obedience to HaShem". Take the lesson of the Pharaoh of Moses seriously, "making a decision against HaShem enough times will result in losing yourself to the Red Sea – PERMANENTLY"

"24 If any man will come after me, let him deny himself, and take up his cross, and follow me 25 For whosoever will save his life shall lose it: and whosoever will lose his life for my sake shall find it." Matthew 16:24, 25. "When the righteous turns from his righteousness, and commits iniquity, he shall even die thereby." Ezekiel 33:18.

(KJ-Revelation) "{4:1} *after this* I looked, and, behold, a door [was] opened in heaven: and the first voice which I heard [was] as it were of a trumpet talking with me; which said, come up hither, and I will shew thee things which must be hereafter. {4:2} and immediately I was in the spirit: and, behold, a throne was set in heaven, and [one] sat on the throne. {4:3} and he that sat was to look upon like a jasper and a sardine stone: and [there was] a rainbow round about the throne, in sight like unto an emerald. {4:4} and round about the throne [were] four and twenty seats: and upon the seats I saw four and twenty elders sitting, clothed in white raiment; and they had on their head's crowns of gold. {4:5} and out of the throne proceeded lightning's and thunderings and voices: and [there were] seven lamps of fire burning before the throne, which are the seven Spirits of God. {4:6} and before the throne [there was] a sea of glass like unto crystal: and in the midst of the throne, and round about the throne, [were] four beasts full of eyes before and behind. {4:7} And the first beast [was] like a lion, and the second beast like a calf, and the third beast had a face as a man, and the fourth beast [was] like a flying eagle. {4:8} and the four beasts had each of them six wings about [him;] and [they were] full of eyes within: and they rest not day and night, saying, Holy, holy, holy, Lord God Almighty, which was, and is, and is to come. {4:9} And when those beasts give glory and honor and thanks to him that sat on the throne, who lives for ever and ever, {4:10} The four and twenty elders fall down before him that sat on the throne, and worship him that lives for ever and ever, and cast their crowns before the throne, saying, {4:11} Thou art worthy, O Lord, to receive glory and honor and power: for thou hast created all things, and for thy pleasure they are and were created."

The words of Chapter 4 of Revelation "And after this" follows Chapters 1 to 3. This shows that so far, Revelation is chronological in nature. One might argue that this statement was made by John, but this implies strongly that John was being shown things in the order that they would take place.

(LXXNT-Revelation) "² immediately I was in the Spirit; and behold, there was situated in heaven a throne, and on the throne, someone sitting. ³ and the one sitting was like (Ezekiel 1:26-28, and there the throne is described as looking like stones similar to here. One wonders if some copyists conformed this passage to the one in Ezekiel. It seems more appropriate to describe a throne in terms of stones rather than a person. Yet the one seated is not human. Some copyists were trying to clarify that it was the one sitting that was like that in appearance. At any rate, the stone carnelian is flesh-colored. One could understand either reading as referring to the one sitting. On the one hand, the rule of "*lectio brevior lectio potior*" favors the shorter reading here. The shorter reading makes fine sense, by simply putting a comma between verses 4:2 and 4:3. It seems reasonable that the longer reading is an added explanatory phrase. On the other hand, the seeming redundancy of the NA27 reading, after v. 2 having just said, "Someone sitting" already, is very Johannine in style) jasper stone ("this stone represented the Tribe of Reuben, the first") and carnelian (Greek, sárdion. Some also render this as Sardius ("this stone represented Benjamin, the last so that from Reuben to Benjamin represented the entire nation"). The English word carnelian is derived from the Latin root *carn*, from which we get *carnal* and *carnivore* and *carne*, and was named that because the stone was flesh-colored. The Oxford dictionary defines carnelian as a flesh-colored, deep red, or reddish-white variety of chalcedony) in appearance. And an aura (This is from the Greek word îris, which can mean rainbow or halo. Webster's second definition of aura is: "a luminous radiation: Nimbus." I didn't like rainbow, since the rainbow by definition includes the whole spectrum of colors, whereas this phenomenon is only various shades of green. Halo is possibly suitable; it's just that the English reader is accustomed to it being only something around the heads of holy people or saints in art. But halo is also used in astronomy) encircles the throne, like emerald in appearance. [4] and in a circle around the throne are twenty-four thrones."

In Daniel 7:9, the Ancient of Days took His seat in the midst of the thrones that were set up. (The thrones were empty in Daniel's time.), and on those thrones, twenty-four elders ("Presbuteros – senior, elder, old man", STRG4245) (Are the 24 elders like those of 1 Chronicles 24:7-18 (the elders in charge of the daily service as set up by David), or are they the 12 apostles of the Lamb, plus the 12 patriarchs of Israel?) dressed in white, and on their heads crowns of gold.

"And from the throne come flashes and sounds and thundering's (Exodus 19:16) And there are seven flaming torches burning before the throne, which are the seven spirits of God, [6] and in front of the throne is like a sea of glass, like crystal. And in between the throne and the circle around the throne are four living beings (The Greek word rendered "living being" is zōion, which is defined in the BAGD lexicon as follows: "Living thing or being, to denote beings that are not human and yet not really animals of the usual kind.") full of eyes, front and back. and the first being is like a lion, and the second being like an ox, and the third being has a human face, and the fourth being is like an eagle in flight. **8** and the four beings, every one of them has six wings each, which are covered completely around with eyes, even inward. And they take no rest day or night, continually saying, "Holy, holy, holy is the Lord God Almighty, who was and who is and who is to come." **9** And whenever the beings give glory and honor and thanks to the one sitting on the throne, to him who lives for ever and ever, **10** the twenty-four elders will fall down before him who sits on the throne, and worship him who lives for ever and ever, and they will place their crowns before the throne, saying, **11** "You are worthy, our Lord and our God, to receive glory and honor and power, for you ("su" is a pronoun) created all things, and for your purpose they exist and were created."

(Masoretic Text-Revelation) "After these things I looked, and, Hinei, a delet ("door") having been opened in Shomayim, the kol harishon [the first voice, 1:10], the voice like a shofar that I heard speaking to me, said, Come up here! And I will show you MAH DI LEHEVE ("what will happen," DANIEL 2:28f) after these things. |2| At once I was in the Ruach Hakodesh, and, Hinei, there in Shomayim stood a Kes ("Throne"), and upon the Kes DEMUT KEMAREH ADAM ("a figure in appearance like a Man," YECHEZKEL 1:26-28), [MELACHIM ALEF 22:19; YESHAYAH 6:1; DANIEL 7:9] |3| And the One sitting there was KEMAREH ("in appearance") like jasper stone and carnelian, and a keshet beanan ("rainbow", BERESHIS 9:16) was around the Kes ("Throne") that looks like an emerald. [YECHEZKEL 1:28] |4| and around the Kes ("Throne") were esrim v'arba'ah kisot ("twenty-four thrones") and on the kisot were sitting esrim v'arba'ah Zekenim ("twenty-four Elders", SHEMOT 12:21), each clothed in lavan ("white"), each wearing a kittel, and on the roshim ("heads") of them, golden atarot ("crowns"). |5| and out of the Kes ("Throne") comes forth lightning and sounds and thunders and there were sheva lapidei eish ("torches of fire") burning before the Kes (Throne), which are the sheva ruchot ("spirits", Revelation 1:4) of Hashem [SHEMOT 19:16; ZECHARYAH 4:2]. |6| and before the Kes (Throne) there was something like a sea of glass, like crystal. And on each side and around the Kes (Throne) there were Arbah Chayyot ("four living beings"), being full of eynayim ("eyes") in front and in back. [YECHEZKEL 1:5] |7| and harishonah ("the first") of HaChayyot ["the living beings", YECHEZKEL 1:10; 1:14] was like an aryeh ("lion"), and hasheniyah ("the second") of HaChayyot ("the living beings") like an egel ("calf"), and hashlishit ("the third") of HaChayyot had the face of a ben Adam (human being), and hareve'it ("fourth") of HaChayyot was like a flying nesher ("eagle") (Ezekiel

1:10 has a similar description: "{1:10} As for the likeness of their faces, they four had the face of a man, and the face of a lion, on the right side: and they four had the face of an ox on the left side; they four also had the face of an eagle.) |8| And the Arba HaChayyot ("four living beings"), each one of them had six wings and they were full of eynayim ("eyes") without and within. And yomam valailah ("day and night"), they do not cease to rest but continue singing, KADOSH, KADOSH, KADOSH, ADONOI TZVAOT the One who was and is and is to come. [YESHAYAH 6:3; YECHEZKEL 1:18; YESHAYAH 6:3] |9| and whenever the Chayyot will give kavod ("glory") and hod ("splendor") and hadar ("majesty") and shevakh ("praise") to the One sitting on the Kes, to Him that Hu Chai ad olemei olamim ("that lives forever and ever"), [Psalms 47:8] |10| Then the esrim v'arba'ah Zekenim fall prostrate before the One sitting on the Kes (Throne) and worship the One that Hu Chai ad olemei olamim ("lives forever and ever") and cast down their atarot ("crowns") before the Kes, saying, [DEVARIM 33:3] |11| Worthy art Thou, Adoneinu and Eloheinu, to receive hod ("honor") and hadar ("splendor") and oz ("power"), because it was your "BARAH" that created all things, and because they existed and came to be by your ratzon ("will"). [BERESHIS 1:1]"

- **Illustration 217.00: Throne of God and Sea of Glass through prophetic images in time:** As each prophet gave a description of the throne of God and the sea of glass, they progress to show the changes in their images. The sea is removed in Revelation 21:1. The throne with wheels suggests that the throne was not yet set in a firm place. In Revelation, the throne no longer has wheels.

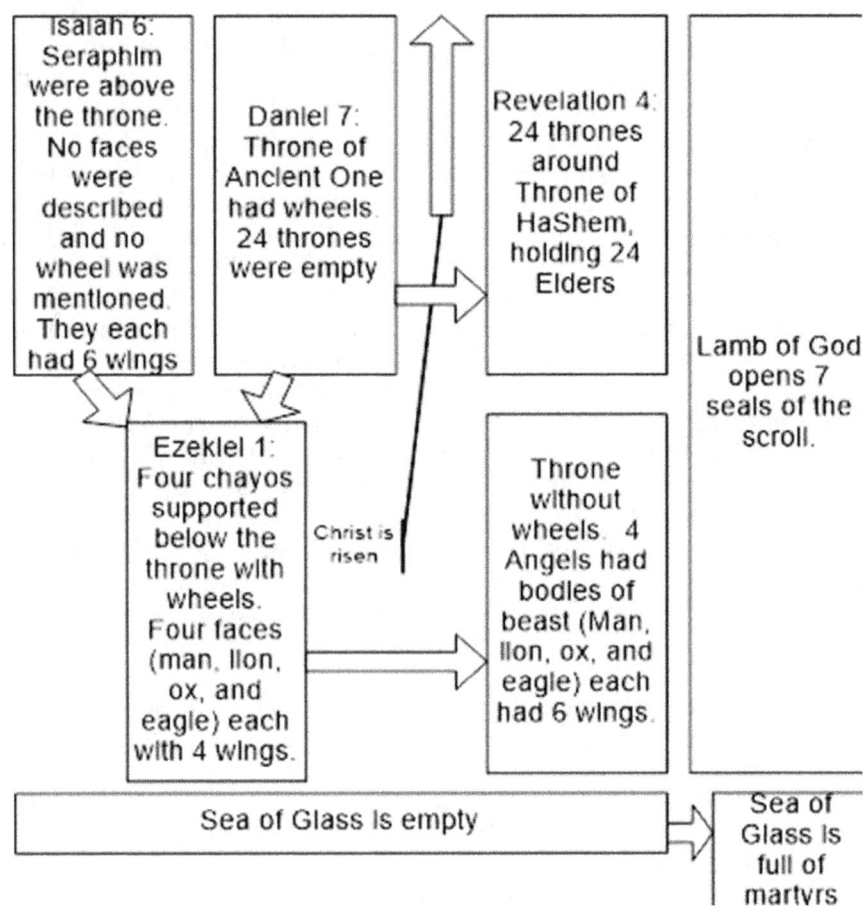

In Daniel 7:9, the 24 thrones are set up but they are empty. This is showing a progression of changes have taken place since Daniel. Now they contain the elders. The Sea of Glass has not yet been filled with the required number of martyrs. Angels never wear crowns or sit on thrones, so these thrones are not meant for angels.

Ezekiel and John both saw the throne of HaShem in their visions. Each of them saws different things taking place around the throne, but they saw the same throne of HaShem. The Sea of Glass before the throne was empty during the time of Ezekiel. It was not empty at the time of John's vision. During the end of John's vision, the sea was full of martyrs. The time of the believer's martyrs had not taken place in the time of Ezekiel, but John was shown the sea after the end of days. One of the seals (seal 5) shall refer to the martyrs crying out for justice.

The 24 thrones were seen as empty in the time of Isaiah, Ezekiel, and Daniel. John saw the thrones containing the 24 elders. By the time of the opening of the first seal, the throne contained the elders and the sea contained the martyrs. The elders that filled the 24 thrones were the pre-Messiah Saints of HaShem that were released from the grave by Yeshua and resurrected on the day that He was resurrected. The 24 elders could not be the Apostles as they have not been resurrected yet at time of the vision. They belong to the saints resurrected on the Second Return. Nor can they be angels who are not allowed to wear crowns. The elders wore the white robes of a priest. Larkin suggests that they are acting priests. This doesn't seem right either as this is the role of Yeshua, who has not yet taken His crown as king.

Most people read Revelation with the idea of learning about what's to come, and what to expect. The main goal of chapter 4 is to show the sovereignty of HaShem, the living transparent God who is willing to share with us His Plan for us to receive His mercy. Verses 9-11 is all one sentence to show that worship is due to Him who sits on the throne.

"{4:9} And when those beasts give glory and honor and thanks to him that sat on the throne, who lives for ever and ever, {4:10} The four and twenty elders fall down before him that sat on the throne, and worship him that lives for ever and ever, and cast their crowns before the throne, saying, {4:11} Thou art worthy, O Lord, to receive glory and honor and power: for thou hast created all things, and for thy pleasure they are and were created."

John is told to enter the door and the voice with a trumpet tells John to "come up here and I will show you what must (this word "must" be imperative and means what is to come is "unavoidable") take place *after these things*. Then John is shown the "Throne of God" with a rainbow around the throne. This takes place after the "seven churches" implying that the messages to the seven churches is about the events before the end times or symbolic of the historical churches. There is nothing more about the churches from here through the rest of Revelation. The words of Yeshua to the churches are "conditional", a warning.

The door having been opened is a perfect passive participle, meaning that the door was opened by (passive voice) God. The word heaven is used more than 50 times in John's writings and is always "singular" except one time; Revelation 12:12.

The words "come up here" have sometimes been miss-interpreted by Dispensationalists as a "secret rapture". They tend to separate the Israelites from the Church. This is a false belief. While there are still some aspects of the coming events that tend toward the Israelites, once Christ was crucified, the Church and Israel became synonymous in HaShem's eyes. There are "believers", there are "believers who do not persevere", and there are "unbelievers". The "true believers" are part of Israel now and as many of the dispersed Israelites became mixed with the nations it is now difficult to tell "true Israelites" from people of different nations. True believers are adopted into the family of Abraham, from which the Israelites originated from. The word "church" does not appear in Revelation after chapter 3 until 22:10. There is nothing to imply that anyone but John was called to "come up here".

# Chapter 12

## Scroll of Revelation

(KJ-Revelation) "{5:1} and I saw in the right hand of him that sat on the throne a book written within and on the backside, sealed with seven seals. {5:2} and I saw a strong ("Ischuros-forceful, powerful, boisterous", STRG2478) angel proclaiming with a loud voice, who is worthy to open the book, and to loosen the seals thereof? {5:3} and no man in heaven, nor in earth, neither under the earth, was able to open the book, neither to look thereon. {5:4} and I wept much, because no man was found worthy to open and to read the book, neither to look thereon. {5:5} and one of the elders saith unto me, weep not: behold, the Lion of the tribe of Juda, the Root of David, hath prevailed to open the book, and to loosen the seven seals thereof. {5:6} And I beheld, and, lo, in the midst of the throne and of the four beasts, and in the midst of the elders, stood a Lamb as it had been slain, having seven horns and seven eyes, which are the seven Spirits of God sent forth into all the earth. {5:7} and he came and took the book out of the right hand of him that sat upon the throne. {5:8} and when he had taken the book, the four beasts and four [and] twenty elders fell down before the Lamb, having every one of them harps, and golden vials full of odors, which are the prayers of saints. {5:9} And they sung a new song, saying, Thou art worthy to take the book, and to open the seals thereof: for thou was slain, and hast redeemed us to God by thy blood out of every kindred, and tongue, and people, and nation; {5:10} And hast made us unto our God kings and priests: and we shall reign on the earth. {5:11} and I beheld, and I heard the voice of many angels round about the throne and the beasts and the elders: and the number of them was ten thousand times ten thousand, and thousands of thousands; {5:12} Saying with a loud voice, Worthy is the Lamb that was slain to receive power, and riches, and wisdom, and strength, and honor, and glory, and blessing."

The "strong" angel is a unique description for an angel, one that has never been used in all the occurrences for an angelic appearance. As strong as this angel was, it was not capable of opening the seals of the scroll.

(MTJ-Revelation 5) "|2| And I saw a strong malach ("angel"), proclaiming in a kol gadol ("loud voice"), who is worthy to open the sefer ("book") and break its chotamot ("seals")?"

(LXXNT-Revelation) "²And I saw a powerful angel, heralding in a loud voice: "Who is worthy to open the scroll, and to break the seals of it?" The Greek word could mean angel with powerful voice: ("Ischuros-forceful, powerful, boisterous", STRG2478).

The lamb stood before the throne, the 24 elders, and the 4 beasts (representing the worldly kingdoms of the world). The lamb had seven horns. Horns have been used in symbolism to represent kings (Horns of the ram, horns of the goat of Greece, and horns of the last empire federation before the "little horn" pops up). This lamb holds the 7 horns that would go forth to all the earth. The lamb is declared to "have redeemed us". This is the last Jubilee of the world before Yeshua becomes king. The Jubilee is indicative of our redemption by the slain lamb: "out of every kindred, and tongue, and people, and nation". The casual reader of the Book of Revelation might not understand the full power and awesomeness of this image.

This is a sevenfold description of the "Lamb".

2. Power
3. Riches
4. Wisdom
5. Strength
6. Honor
7. Glory
8. Blessing
9. There are 5 songs in Revelation 4 and 5:
10. 4:1 Elohim's creative power.
11. 4:8 Song of adoration
12. 5:9 New Song by the Believers
13. 5:12 Song by the messengers
14. 5:13 Song sung by whole creation.

(LXXNT-Revelation) "And I saw upon the right hand of the one sitting on the throne a scroll, written on, inside and back, (Daniel 12:4, 9 "{12:9} And he said, go thy way, Daniel: for the words [are] closed up and sealed till the time of the end") sealed up with seven seals. ² And I saw a powerful angel, heralding in a loud voice: "Who is worthy to open the scroll, and to break the seals of it?" ³

And no one was able, not in heaven nor on the earth nor under the earth, to open the scroll, or even to look at it. ⁴ And I was weeping greatly, that no one worthy was found, to open the scroll, or even to look at it. ⁵ Then one of the elders is saying to me, "Do not weep. Look, the Lion of the tribe of Judah, the Root of David (Christ), he has *overcome* (used in the chapters 2 and 3 about the churches), so as to open the scroll and the seven seals of it." ⁶ And I saw in between the throne and the four living beings and the elders, a lamb, postured as though slain, having seven horns and seven eyes, which are the [seven] spirits of God sent forth into all the earth (Zechariah 4:10: "4:10 For who has despised the day of small things? For these seven shall rejoice, and shall see the plummet in the hand of Zerubbabel; *these are* the eyes of Yehovah, which run to and fro through the whole earth."). ⁷ And he went and took *the scroll* from the right hand of the One sitting on the throne. ⁸ And when he had taken the scroll, the four living beings and the twenty-four elders fell down before the Lamb, each one holding a lyre and a golden bowl filled with incenses, which are the prayers of the saints, ⁹ and they began singing a new song, saying: "You are worthy to take the scroll, and to open the seals of it, because you were slain, and thereby purchased some (variants of LXXNT might be: 1. purchased for God, 2. purchased for God us, 3. purchased us, 4. purchased us for God,  or 5. purchased us for God our ) for God with your blood out of every tribe and language and people and nation!" ¹⁰ "And you made them into a kingdom and priesthood for our God, and they will reign on the earth." ¹¹ And I looked, and I heard the voices of many angels encircled around the throne, and of the living beings and of the elders, and the number of them was ten thousand times ten thousand and thousands upon thousands, ¹² saying with a very great voice, "Worthy is the Lamb that was slain, to receive power and riches and wisdom and strength and honor and glory and blessing!" ¹³ and every creature that was in heaven, and on the earth, and under the earth, and in the sea, and all the things that were in them, I heard saying, "Blessing and honor, glory and power, be to Him who sits on the throne, and to the Lamb, for ever and ever!" ¹⁴ and the four beings were saying "Amen." And the elders fell down and worshiped."

Seeing the lamb "able" to take the book from the right hand of the Almighty was enough for them to know the lamb was to be worshipped.

(MTJ-Daniel 12) "|4| But thou, O Daniel, shut up the devarim ("words"), and seal the sefer ("scroll or book"), until the Et Ketz

("Time of the End"): rabbim shall run to and fro, that da'as ("knowledge") may be increased."

(MTJ-Revelation) "And I saw on the yamin ("right hand") of the One sitting on the Kes (Throne) a sefer ("book, scroll, rolled book", STRG975) (Daniel 12:4 "{12:4} But thou, O Daniel, shut up the words, and seal the book, [even] to the time of the end: many shall run to and fro, and knowledge shall be increased" and Ezekiel 2:9 "{2:9} And when I looked, behold, an hand [was] sent unto me; and, lo, a roll of a book [was] therein;".

Isaiah 29:11 "{29:11} And the vision of all is become unto you as the words of a book that is sealed, which [men] deliver to one that is learned, saying, Read this, I pray thee: and he saith, I cannot; for it [is] sealed") having been written inside and on the back, having been sealed with sheva chotamot ("seven seals"). [YECHEZKEL 2:9, 10; YESHAYAH 29:11; DANIEL 12:4] |2| And I saw a strong malach ("angel"), proclaiming in a kol gadol ("loud voice"), who is worthy to open the sefer ("book") and break its chotamot ("seals")? |3| and no one in Shomayim or on ha'aretz or under ha'aretz was being able to open the sefer ("book") or to look into it. |4| And I was weeping copiously because no one was found worthy to open the sefer (book) or to look into it. |5| And one of the Zekenim says to me, Do not weep, Hinei, HaAryeh ("The Lion") from the Shevet Yehudah ("Tribe of Judah" - Genesis 49:9 "{49:9} Judah [is] a lion's whelp"), the Shoresh Dovid ("*Root of Dovid*"), has won the nitzachon ("victory") and he is able to open the sefer ("book") and its sheva chotamot ("seven seals"). [BERESHIS 49:9; YESHAYAH 11:1, 10] |6| And I saw between the Kes (Throne) and the Arbah Chayyot ("four living beings") and among the Zekenim (Elders, SHEMOT 12:21) a SEH ("Lamb", *YESHAYAH 53:7, Moshiach*) having stood as having been slain, having sheva karnayim ("horns", -*omnipotence*), sheva eynayim ("eyes", -*omniscience*), which are the sheva ruchot (spirits) of Hashem having been sent into kol ha'aretz (all the earth). |7| And the SEH ("Lamb", YESHAYAH 53:7) came and has taken the sefer out of the yamin (right hand) of the One sitting on the Kes ("Throne"). |8| And when the SEH ("lamb") (YESHAYAH 53:7) received the sefer, the Arbah Chayyot ("four living beings") and the esrim v'arba'ah Zekenim ("twenty-four Elders", SHEMOT 12:21) fell down before the SEH, ("Lamb", YESHAYAH 53:7) each one having a nevel ("harp") and golden ke'arot ("bowls") full of ketoret ("incense"), which are the tefillos ("prayers") of the Kadoshim ("saints"). [Psalms 141:2; 16:3] |9| and they are singing a SHIR CHADASH (Psalms 96:1) saying, Worthy art thou to take the sefer (book) and to open the chotamot (seals) of it, because you were slain and with your dahm [kapporah blood] you paid the price for the Geulah [VAYIKRA 25:50 51] redemption and purchased ones for Hashem from every mishpochah ("family") and lashon ("tongue") and am ("people") and goy ("nation"), [TEHILLIM 40:3; 98:1; YESHAYAH 42:10] |10| And made them for Eloheinu a Malchut and kohanim, and they will reign on ha'aretz ("the earth"). |11| And I saw and I heard the kol ("voice") of many malachim ("angels"); they numbered myriads of myriads and v'alfei alafim ("thousands of thousands"), around the Kes (Throne) and the Chayyot ("the living beings") and the Zekenim ("Elders", SHEMOT 12:21) [DANIEL 7:10] |12| Saying with a kol gadol ("loud or strong voice"), Worthy is the SEH ("Lamb", *SHEMOT 12:3; YESHAYAH 53:7 Moshiach*) having been slain, to receive the oz ("power") and the osher ("wealth") and the chochmah ("wisdom") and the gevurah ("strength") and hod ("honor") and kavod ("glory") and bracha ("blessing"). |13| And every beriyah ("creature") which is in Shomayim and on ha'aretz ("the earth") and under ha'aretz and on the yam ("sea") and all things in them, I heard saying, To the One sitting on the Kes ("Throne") and to the SEH ("Lamb", *SHEMOT 12:3; YESHAYAH 53:7 Moshiach*) be the bracha ("blessing") and the hod ("honor") and the hadar ("glory") and the memshalah ("dominion") and Olemei Olamim ("Amen Amens") ("forever and ever"). [DIVREY HAYAMIM ALEF 29:11; MALACHI 1:6; 2:2] |14| And the Arbah Chayyot were saying, Omein. And the Zekenim (Elders, SHEMOT 12:21) fell down and worshiped."

This chapter makes clear that there is only ONE Savior righteous to open the seals, ONE Savior for the world. This contradicts a "two earth theory or Gap theory of Genesis 1:1-2 as there would have been no savior for a previous "earth". It is also contradictory of other planets having human like life forms as they would have no Savior.

The "book" or "scroll" is sealed. Daniel and Isaiah both mention the book that is sealed until the end. Daniel was told about the events of the end, but as the seals are unlocked, events unfold that were not told to Isaiah or Daniel. The scroll was in the "Right Hand" of God. This was the Hand of God that worked the History of mankind for the "creation week of history". God's grace and long-suffering has come to an end. Now is the time of justice, not mercy. It was written on "both" sides meaning the "fullness of the judgments to come". God's purpose will be fulfilled. These judgments will lead into the final Kingdom and defeat Satan's kingdom, restoring the kingdom of Earth under the authority of

God and the King of Kings. This is an indirect reference to the Yovel as that is exactly what the Yovel is about, redemption and restoring the original owner of the earth back to power.

The order of the seals is chronological. There is a telescopic order: Seals One to Six → Seventh seal → Trumpets → Seventh Trumpet → Bowls → Seventh Bowl finalizes HaShem's judgment. This scroll confirms the idea that HaAdam lost his lordship over the earth to Satan in Genesis. The phrase in the Greek: "Sealed up with seven seals." "Sealed up" is katasfragizw from kata meaning "down" and sfragizw, "to seal." This compound verb means "tightly sealed, firmly sealed," and so, "very hidden, very secure." The number seven means perfect completion in God's perspective. All the seals must be broken for the scroll to be read. The scrolls must be opened in a successive order to be read and the successive order that they were sealed.

The words Amen Amens confirm that it is finalized that the Lamb of God will be able to open the seals. The second Hebrew word for Amen is plural: "Olamim". This makes the translation literally "Amen Amens". It has been clarified by Joseph ben Jacob that 2 is the number of confirmations, which means that this Amen has been set in stone.

The Roman custom of making a *will* included a ceremony involving a testator and seven witnesses. For each of the *seven witnesses there was a seal*. In addition, a very reliable friend was selected who would, for a coin, purchase the property for the family. In this way the property would become the property of the reliable friend, however, upon the death of the testator, the very reliable friend would return the property to the rightful heirs. For such a document, a long scroll of parchment was used. The writer of the document would begin writing and after a period, he would stop, roll up the parchment enough to cover his words, and then seal the scroll with wax. He would then resume writing, stop, seal another portion, and so on until the entire scroll was sealed with seven seals. In this way, the scroll would read a section at a time after each seal was broken.

In the analogy, the Lord Jesus is the reliable "Friend" who has purchased our redemption and is here seen opening the seals which provide us with our inheritance. In this case, He is reclaiming that which was lost by Adam. Further, this procedure was used to keep unauthorized persons from opening the seven-sealed scroll.

Only a "worthy" person, the one with the right credentials, could open the seals, read the inheritance, and give it to the inheritors. No one was "capable" of opening the seals other than the Lamb of God.

The Jewish Custom refers back to the Yovel. If a Jewish family were to lose its property or possessions by some kind of misfortune or distress, their property could not be permanently taken from them (the Old Testament law of jubilee and the kinsman redeemer protected them against this). Their losses were listed in a scroll and sealed seven times. Then the conditions necessary to purchase back the land and their possessions were written on the outside of the scroll. When a qualified redeemer could be found, who could meet the requirements of reclamation (a kinsman like Boaz as in the story of Ruth), the one who had taken the property was required to return it to the original owner. Daniel was ordered to close and seal the book just as one would for a Yovel document or a testament with "seven seals" A twofold picture of Christ is offered.

- **Contrasting description of Yeshua:** The two pictures here given of Christ.

| Jesus as the Lion | Jesus as the Lamb (standing as if slain with 7 eyes and 7 horns) |
|---|---|
| the lion character refers to His second coming | the lamb character refers to His first coming (His ministry on earth) |
| the lion speaks of His majesty | the lamb speaks of His humility |
| as lion He is sovereign | as lamb He is Savior |
| as lion He is Judge | as lamb He is judged in our place |
| the lion speaks of the government of God | the lamb speaks of the grace of God |

The word "standing" is a perfect tense of the verb "to stand". He had been slain, but now He is seen "not dead", but the marks of His having been "slain" are definitely still there. The horn is a symbol of power, as is shown in the beasts of Daniel. Seven horns refer to a "perfect government" that will follow. The seven eyes refer to his unlimited wisdom and insight. He takes the scroll out of the right hand of the Ancient One. Who can take anything out of the right hand of HaShem?

Daniel declares, "I saw in the night visions, and, behold, *one* like the Son of man came with the clouds of heaven, and came to the Ancient of days, and they brought him near before him. And there was given him dominion, and glory, and a kingdom, that all people, nations, and languages, should serve him: his dominion *is* an everlasting dominion, which shall not pass away, and his kingdom *that* which shall not be destroyed."

The "Right hand" or the right side, or right limb, of a person receives special prominence; the place of honor is at his right. "Upon thy right hand did stand the queen" (Psalms 45: 9). Solomon placed a seat of honor for his mother, the queen, on his right side (I Kings 2: 19). The right eye was the most important and most vital member of the body. Nahash the Ammonite, as a reproach upon all Israel, purposed putting out the right eye of all men in Jabesh-gilead (I Samuel 11: 2).

With the introduction of the scroll, the Wrath of God is also introduced. The Dead Sea Scroll (Q390) contains a reference to the last jubilee before the week where Belial rules. During this Jubilee, people will turn completely to wickedness and break all of the commandments (which is being experienced in our current years). Up to this point, there have been many signs that this time was coming. Many of those signs were given in the Gospels and the Letters of the Apostles. These signs appeared in the previous 50 years during the beginning of the end times. The amazing thing is that the Christians on earth, many who do not understand that this is a time for the Wrath of God, will witness the events that take place. They will wonder why HaShem is doing such terrible things upon the earth and many will "lose faith".

(Luke) {21:11} and great earthquakes shall be in divers' places, and famines, and pestilences; and fearful sights and great signs shall there be from heaven. {21:12} But before all these, they shall lay their hands on you, and persecute [you,] delivering [you] up to the synagogues, and into prisons, being brought before kings and rulers for my name's sake. {21:13} and it shall turn to you for a testimony.

Many churches do not wish to believe that HaShem will leave His people on earth during the events of the tribulation. They teach that the Christians will not have to suffer during this time. If one reads the seals carefully, it would be easy to see that many of the plagues do not apply to those with the *Mark of God* on their forehead.  Why would HaShem bother with a "mark of God" on believers if they were not going to be here anyway?

It is foolish to believe that there will be no martyrs in the end time. One of the seals concerns the martyrs and how HaShem is waiting for the *number of martyrs to be fulfilled*. This means that there will be martyrs at the end of the tribulation and that means that Christians or Believers will be here at that time. The common belief is that these believers or martyrs are the ones who believed *after* the rapture had taken place, but this belief has another problem in that it requires *two* raptures, one for us regular folk (usually believed to take place before the tribulation) and one for late martyrs of the Tribulation. There is nothing to suggest that there will be two raptures.

# Chapter 13

## The rapture

The subject of the date of Yeshua's return is a subject of very high debate and concern. There have been many calculations about when Yeshua Messiah would return, and most of them have been wrong. The Jehovah Witness Church has calculated several dates, all of them have passed showing that their calculations are in error.

The predictions about the Second Coming have taken place for over a thousand years. Just before the turn of the millennium (1000 CE), many thoughts that it was time for the return. During the time of Napoleon Bonaparte in France and during the time of Hitler many thought that the Anti-Christ had come and it was the time of the end. Many thoughts that the change of the more recent millennium (2000 CE) would be the time of the end. This last one assumes that our Julian\Gregorian calendar matches with the calendar of HaShem.

The problem, with these predictions, is that they didn't take into account many of the prophecies about the end times from Jeremiah, Ezekiel, and Daniel. There were many facets missing. The predictions before and during Hitler didn't taken into account the return and restoration of the Jewish nation, which took place *after World War II ended*. This was predicted strongly by Ezekiel (Ezekiel 34-39) and was a strong indicator of the end times or ends of days. The Temple has yet to be rebuilt (as of this writing) and this is necessary before Satan can violate the Temple with the Desolation.

At this time, many take the words of Yeshua too far when He said that no one knows the *day or the hour of His return save the Father*. This verse has strong relevance to the calendar in use by the Hebrews. It says nothing about not knowing the month or year of the return, only the day and the hour! It is dangerous to "add words" to what Yeshua actually said. (I know, I know... a double negative but in this case the double negative clarifies the point.)

With this there are several theories presented about the return of Yeshua according to the plan of HaShem and the time table of the fulfillment of the work of HaShem. HaShem told us in the symbolism of the creation process that His work would take 6000 years (assuming that the figurative language of the creation week holds for each day representing 1000 years). Given that Yeshua was crucified in year 4000 AT this leads us to know that His Return will take place in the year 6000 AT (by MT dating). Year 6000 AT is matched to the year 2037 CE using MT dating of the Bible (at this time, LXX dating is being ignored due to the explained problems with LXX dates). This is 2000 years exactly (40 Yovel cycles) from the crucifixion which took place in 4000 A.T. The 40 Yovel Cycles is related to the life of Moses who had 3 periods of 40 years representing the 40 Yovel Cycles.

The problem is that we don't know *for sure* when He was crucified. This work *proposes* year 37 CE, but that date is based on the combination of Daniel, Ezra, and extra-Biblical evidence concerning the rulers of Persia. Nothing in the Bible guarantees year 37 CE as the year of the crucifixion. Other factors must be taken into account to know the year of the Return.

The restoration of the Jewish nation is another factor that can be used to indicate the year of the return. With the dual exile period of Jeremiah, it has already been discussed about the restoration of the Jews taking a dual time period as well. The first restoration time period started in 1948 CE. Adding 70 years to this takes us to 2018 CE. The second mirrored time period started in 1967 CE when *Jerusalem* was captured by Israel and reestablished for the first time since its destruction in 70 CE Adding 70 years to this year, places the end of the Jewish restoration in 2037 CE. This supports the 6000-year plan and the 2000 years from the crucifixion that have been proposed as time tables of HaShem.

The Second Return of Yeshua will take place on one of the feasts of the Laws of Moses. The very essence of the Feasts of the Law of Moses was Messiah centered. It has already been discussed about the events of Yeshua's life having taken place during feasts of the year as He "fulfilled the law". The only feast or event left unmatched to the events of His life is His Second Return and Rosh Hashanah, which falls on Tishrei 1. This chronology wishes to step out with the proposal that the Return will take place in Tishrei, due to the remaining feast left unattached to any major event in Yeshua's life.

The Hebrew calendar operates in such a way that each year has to be calculated based on the year before and the year after. The reason for this is the calculation of short or long years and to keep 2 Shabbats from occurring next to each other. A day can be added or subtracted depending on the year before and after. With the addition of the 4 rules to the Metonic calendar, *no one knows the day or hour when Tishrei 1 will fall each year until that year comes!* This is strongly relevant to what Yeshua said. No one can know the "day or the hour" when the calendar starts each year so no one can know the exact day of Rosh Hashanah in the year 6000 AT.

Due to the earth's revolutionary changes during the days of Hezekiah, the *exact day count cannot be calculated with any degree of accuracy.* No 2 calendar algorithms return the same day count for long periods of time. This means that the date of Tishrei 1 in our current calculations may not be the correct date according to the calculations of Hashem our God. If anyone is concerned that an attempt has been made (here) to "predict" the day of the return, they can rest assured that *it isn't possible* to do such a prediction with even a small chance of accuracy. Any suggested date given here is a best guess scenario.

Before 715 BC, this wasn't true. With a calendar of 360 days per year *exactly*, the day count up to the year 6000 AT could have been calculated with a good degree of dependability. The changes taking place in 715 BC destroyed this capability *by God's design.* Hezekiah had no clue as to the overall repercussions of the "sign he asked of Isaiah". The day count from creation up to Nissan 1, 3249 AT MT (Hezekiah's year 14) = 1,169,280 which is exactly 167,040 full 7-day weeks or 38,976 full 30-day months.

Day counts were dropped from the date portion of the chronology in this work after 715 BC due to the inaccuracy of such counts. This throws a huge monkey wrench in to the modern-day theologians who attempt to match ancient prophecies of the Prophets with modern times. CANNOT BE DONE accurately. Does this need repeating? Modern day theologians cannot possibly match the dates of ancient prophecies with accurate modern-day dates.

Given this the *proposed date* of the Second Return is on Tishrei 1, 6000 AT or Tishrei 1, 2037 CE The matching Gregorian date is even more obtuse and cannot be accurately calculated against the current Hebrew calendar. The Hebrew calendar places a year of 5798 AM on the year that is matched to 6000 AT. Since the calendar years differ, the Hebrew calendar calculations can't be used to calculate the proposed date. This leaves us with a proposed date that *is relatively useless and validates the statement of Christ in that no man knows the day or the hour.*

We can look for the time when it approaches according to certain events predicted (which is what Yeshua told us to do), but that's as close as can be attained to knowing the *actual date of the Second Return* and "No man knows the Day or the Hour of His return except the father."

# Chapter 14

## Tribulation Interpretation and Opening of the Seals

The most common interpretation of Revelation is that all the seals (trumpets and vials included) of the Scroll are opened within a 7-year period called the Tribulation or the Week of Jacob's Trouble.

Not taken into account is the fact that these are all opened *before Satan is cast out of heaven for the last time in the middle of the 7-year period of the Tribulation* if one is to believe that Revelation is given in chronological order. This doesn't necessarily present a problem in that they simply "move the event of Satan being cast out" placing these verses in the middle of the opening of the seals. This interpretation is accompanied by the understanding that the events in Revelation are not necessarily in chronological order. That is not the interpretation here!

A chronological interpretation by this theory of Revelation means that the seals, trumpets, and vials must all take place in the first 3 and a half years, not 7 unless Revelation is not chronological. This comes with an entire new set of problems. For instance, the seal that unleashes famine and disease (seal 4) strikes one fourth of the population. Since there were 3 seals before this, this doesn't give much time for people to die of starvation and disease in 1 or less years and this must go along with the issues of the other seals, trumpets, and vials. There are 2 major earthquakes; one between seal 5 and 6 and an even bigger earthquake in the silence between seal 6 and 7.

The Second Coming of Yeshua causes issues with this interpretation as well. He is the ONLY one who can open the seals and to do that *He must be in heaven with the scroll*. Pre-tribulation Rapture believers and Mid-Tribulation Rapture believers would have to believe that after the Rapture, He returns to heaven, but NOTHING tells us this takes place. After the Rapture, He becomes King of Kings to bring in the Millennial Kingdom. He can't be King here and open the seals up there as the "slain lamb of God".

Finally, nothing about this interpretation takes into account the Kinsman Redeemer facet of Christ. If the scroll is opened by the mid-tribulation (before Satan is cast out), then this belies Him redeeming the earth and mankind on a Yovel year. This interpretation totally ignores the Yovel nature of Christ's redeeming act.

God can do anything He wants. It is possible that He might make all the seal openings take place quickly (within a 3- or 7-year limit) as described in the seals, yet the nuances of the wording in Revelation alludes to another interpretation of opening the seals; that of taking an entire Yovel Cycle (Yovel Cycle number 120 - a number common to types of Noah and Moses) to open the seals. This means that each seal is opened (in chronological order of Revelation) during one week of years within this last Yovel Cycle: (The Julian Calendar is not an absolute interpretation, but is a suggested time by the Julian\Gregorian calendar.)

- Seal 1 - 5951 - 5957 A.T. by MT; 7375 - 7381 A.T. by LXX; and 1988 - 1994 C.E. By Julian calendar. This is week 1 of the Yovel.
- Seal 2 - 5958 - 5964 A.T. by MT; 7382 - 7388 A.T. by LXX; and 1995 - 2001 C.E. By Julian calendar. This is week 2 of the Yovel.
- Seal 3 - 5965 - 5971 A.T. by MT; 7389 - 7395 A.T. by LXX; and 2002 - 2008 C.E. By Julian calendar. This is week 3 of the Yovel.
- Seal 4 - 5972 - 5978 A.T. by MT; 7396 - 7402 A.T. by LXX; and 2009 - 2015 C.E. By Julian calendar. This is week 4 of the Yovel.
- Seal 5 - 5979 - 5985 A.T. by MT; 7403 - 7409 A.T. by LXX; and 2016 - 2022 C.E. By Julian calendar. This is week 5 of the Yovel.
- Seal 6 - 5986 - 5992 A.T. by MT; 7410 - 7416 A.T. by LXX; and 2023 - 2929 C.E. By Julian calendar. This is week 6 of the Yovel.
- Seal 7 - 5993 - 5999 A.T. by MT; 7417 - 7423 A.T. by LXX; and 2930 - 2936 C.E. By Julian calendar: This seal becomes the Tribulation Week by this interpretation.

The seals might not be limited to "their" week, but may extend throughout the length of the following seals. Seal 3 is an example: This seal is telling us that the price of food will skyrocket and food will cost most of "a day's pay". While this was strong during week 3 of years, it did not necessarily "end" with that week but continues throughout seals 4 through 7.

It might be noted that the word "rapture" cannot be found anywhere in the Bible and is a word created by modern theologians, divinity professors, and Church leaders to mean "the harvest of believers". But, the word "Bible" cannot be found anywhere in the Bible either.

The word "Rapture" in English, comes from the Latin word raptus ("a carrying off"). The Greek is "harpazo", which means "snatching away with an intensive force", which appears in 1 Thessalonians 4: 17 (and Matt 11: 12, 13: 19, Acts 8: 39, 23: 10, Rev 12: 5 and many other places).

The Rapture of the Church would require that He leave heaven and meet His Bride halfway as dictated throughout the scriptures, and typified by Isaac when he went to meet Rebecca halfway through the field.

Given this, there are a few basic theories or beliefs about when the rapture will take place in relationship to the Tribulation.

- **Pre-tribulation:** This theory proposes that the "Rapture" will take place at the beginning of the opening of the First seal of the scroll or just before. Bride will be removed from the earth before the Tribulation start for the entire Tribulation period up to chapter 19, then they will return with Y'shua for Armageddon. With the Bride of Christ staying in Heaven during the entire Tribulation, she will fulfill the Shabua (period of 7) mentioned in Rev 3: 10.

This belief is particularly popular with most churches as it is hoped that the believers would not have to suffer the events of the tribulation. Many believe in a "pre-tribulation" rapture of the living and dead saints of Christ. This message does not support that, but serves to guide us that believers will be here for the "hour of trial", but He will protect those who remain faithful from this hour.

"I in turn will guard you from that hour of trial which is soon coming upon the whole world, to put to the test the inhabitants of the earth. 11 I am coming quickly: cling to that which you already possess, so that your wreath of victory be not taken away from you."

Or in the MTJ: "I will also be shomer over you, guarding you from the sha'at hanisayon ("hour of trial") about to come upon the Olam Hazeh, to try all the ones of the inhabited world, all the ones dwelling upon the earth."

Pre-tribulation rapture requires that Yeshua must return to heaven to open the seals after the rapture as He must open the seals and He must meet His bride halfway for the rapture.

Pre-tribulation according to the Yovel interpretation: In this scenario, the first 6 seals have been opened (a total of 42 years having passed). The rapture takes place at the beginning of "seal 7" after the Lamb of God has opened seal 7. The events of this seal take place over 7 years, which is the time of the Tribulation.

The Messianic Believers are spared from the events of the "anti-Christ rule, the 7 trumpets, and the horrible events of the vials. While the seven-year Tribulation period is taking place on earth, the bride will be hidden (concealed) from the sight of those living on the earth. Y'shua is a Jew and will marry His bride in the Ancient.

(KJ-Psalm 27:5): "{27:5} for in the time of trouble he shall hide me in his pavilion: in the secret of his tabernacle shall he hide me; he shall set me up upon a rock."

With the 7 seals opened, Christ is now free to claim His throne and His crown as the King of the Messianic Age (1000 years).

- **Mid-Tribulation:** The rapture will take place half way through the Tribulation (this is to be interpreted as the midpoint of the opening of the 7 scrolls). The rapture takes place around 3 and a half years through the tribulation. For the 7-year interpretation of the opening of the scrolls, this takes place around the same time that Satan is cast out of heaven. This one is not popular as it comes with problems.

Once again it requires that Christ leave His post in heaven from opening the seals to meet the Bride halfway and then return to Heaven to finish opening the seals. There is nothing in Revelation that speaks to Christ taking a break from opening the seals to retrieve His Bride.

- **Armageddon Rapture**: The Bride stays for the entire period on the earth until YHWH's time of wrath. They will then be raptured and return with Y'shua for Armageddon. With the Bride's stay on earth during part of the Tribulation, she will be fully protected. The Tribulation period for them is seven years; and others in this group say only three and a half years.

- **Post-Tribulation**: The rapture will take place at the end of the Tribulation (to be interpreted as after seal 7 has been opened and after the 7 trumpets and the vials). The Bride stays for the entire period on the earth up to chapter 19 of Revelation and only then they will be Raptured and return with Y'shua for Armageddon. With her stay on earth during the entire Tribulation, she will be fully protected. The Tribulation period for some is seven years; and others in this group is three and a half years (Jacobs Trouble, Jeremiah 30: 7; Dan 12: 1).

- **Pre-Tribulation according to the Yovel interpretation**: In this scenario, the first 6 seals have been opened (a total of 42 years having passed). The rapture takes place at the beginning of "seal 7" after the Lamb of God has opened seal 7. The events of this seal take place over 7 years, which is equal to the time of the Tribulation.

The Messianic Believers are spared from the events of the "anti-Christ rule, the 7 trumpets, and the horrible events of the vials. While the seven-year Tribulation period is taking place on earth, the bride will be hidden (concealed) from the sight of those living on the earth. Y'shua is a Jew and will marry His bride in the Ancient.

(KJ-Psalm 27:5): "{27:5} for in the time of trouble he shall hide me in his pavilion: in the secret of his tabernacle shall he hide me; he shall set me up upon a rock."

With the 7 seals opened, Christ is now free to claim His throne and His crown as the King of the Messianic Age (1000 years).

- **Post-Tribulation according to the Yovel interpretation of the seals**: This is pretty much the same as 221.04.

The problems with the first four theories is that they take place before seal 5 is opened, and it clearly says during this seal that those slain for the word of God have to "wait a little while and why would they need the Mark of God if they are not on earth to suffer the trials:" for the number of martyrs to be complete, meaning that there are more martyrs to come. This presents a problem if the "rapture" has already taken place. When do these special people get raptured, if the rapture has already taken place? There is nothing to suggest that "another or second" rapture will take place." This does not present any problem for theories the other theories.

(KJ) "{7:13} and one of the elders answered, saying unto me, what are these which are arrayed in white robes? And whence came they? {7:14} and I said unto him, Sir, thou know. And he said to me, these are they which came out of great tribulation, and have washed their robes, and made them white in the blood of the Lamb. {7:15} therefore are they before the throne of God, and serve him day and night in his temple: and he that sits on the throne shall dwell among them."

In the different theories above, there are events that need to be taken into account in the chronology of the End of Days:

Two witnesses spend 3 and 1\2 years on earth.

Two witnesses are taken up after their time.

The anti-Christ makes contract of peace with Israel for 7 years.

The anti-Christ breaks the contract after 3 1\2 years and the Abomination of Desolation.

Lucifer is cast out of heaven along with 1\3 of the angels who follow him halfway through Tribulation week.

The harvest of the wheat and tares by the angels with sickles.

Yeshua becomes King of Kings for the next 1000 years.

# Chapter 15

# Opening the Seals

**First Seal; White Horse:** (KJ-Revelation) "{6:1} and I saw when the Lamb opened one of the seals, and I heard, as it were the noise of thunder, one of the four beasts saying, Come and see ("⁷ And the first being is like a lion"). {6:2} and I saw, and behold a white horse: and he that sat on him had a bow; and a crown was given unto him: and he went forth conquering, and to conquer."

(LXXNT-Revelation) "¹ And I watched as ("saw that") the Lamb opened the first of the seven seals. And I heard one of the four living beings saying in a thunderous voice, "Come." ² And I looked, and behold, a white horse, and the one sitting on it holding a bow, and to him was given a crown, and he went out conquering ("nikao-to overcome, subdue, conquer, to get victory", STRG3528) and to conquer."

(MTJ-Revelation) "And I saw when the SEH ("Lamb", *SHEMOT 12:3; YESHAYAH 53:7 Moshiach*) opened one of the sheva chotamot ("seven seals"). And I heard one of the Arbah Chayyot ("four living beings") saying, as with a voice of thunder, "Come and see! |2| And I saw, and, Hinei, a sus lavan ("white horse"), and the one sitting on it having a keshet ("bow", YECHEZKEL 39:3) and was given to him an atarah, ("diadem") and he went forth conquering, intent on conquest."

(JPS-Revelation) "1 And when the Lamb broke one of the seven seals I saw it, and I heard one of the four living creatures say, as if in a voice of thunder, "Come." 2 And I looked and a white horse appeared, and its rider carried a bow; and a victor's wreath was given to him; and he went out conquering and in order to conquer."

This doesn't say seal number 1, but it is the first seal to be opened.

(LV-Revelation) "2 And I saw: and behold a white horse, and he that sat on him had a bow, and there was a crown given him, and he went forth conquering that he might conquer."

In Revelation 19 Christ came riding on a white horse, but this white horse could not be Christ. Christ is still in heaven to open the other seals. The rider had a bow, but no arrows. He came to conquer, but he was not equipped to win the battle yet but to "rule". It says he was "intent on conquering". The white horse could mean that this rider has the *"appearance" of being good*, but in reality, has nefarious purposes, especially concerning "Messianic Believers" (which includes both Jews and Christians). Yeshua comes with a "sword", not a bow. The rider has no arrows, because he will come in "peace" to deceive the elect or he has no power to really conquer.

Jeremiah 50 refers to Babylon as having a bow without arrows and Babylon is represented by a lion. Ezekiel 39:3 states that HaShem will "{39:3} and I will smite thy bow out of thy left hand, and will cause thine arrows to fall out of thy right hand." This verse suggests that this rider has been smitten so the arrows fell out of his right hand per Ezekiel. The diadem or crown suggests that this rider has the appearance of a ruler or king.

When the seal was broken, it was "one of the living creatures" who spoke to John to come. It does not say which of the living creatures spoke. He went out to "get victory" but it does not indicate that he got victory yet. He could be a ruler come to instigate war but not actually being a part of that war or having lost the war. If the rider of the white horse is not the Anti-Christ, then it remains a big question as to who is able to wear a crown and bear the bow. The angels are not allowed to wear crowns, so it cannot be an angel. The crown bearer must be someone who bears a kingly title or a position of leadership.

Clarence Larkin interprets that the rider is the Anti-Christ. He wears a crown and carries a bow, but no arrow, meaning he has the ruler ship, but not yet the means to carry out his devices and schemes. This is contradicted by the fact that the anti-Christ comes from the pit later on in Revelation.

Many theologians try to "guesstimate" who this rider is. He might be this or he might be that, but in truth, the answer has not been revealed to us yet.

By the Yovel theory of opening the seals, this rider has come already and yet there is still no indication of who he is. By theory 1, this is the anti-Christ coming to power at the beginning of the Tribulation week but still not having the power to completely conquer. It says he came conquering but there is no real indication that he brought death or disease. No one seemed to suffer for his appearance.

If all the seals are all opened during the week of the Tribulation (Theory 1), then this is the beginning of that Tribulation as this is year 1 of the 7 years. But this rider clearly does not have the instruments to rule as the anti-Christ yet.

Theory 2 purports the idea that this seal was opened in the week 1 of the last Yovel Cycle 5951 – 5957 AT by MT; 7375-7381 AT by LXX; and estimated 1988 – 1994 CE by Julian.

- **Anti-Christ:** The Bible never specifically refers to the coming leader as the "Antichrist".

Anti-Christ purposes to anti-duplicate the ministry of Yeshua. That is, the ministry or leadership of the Anti-Christ is to take place over 7 years. This is confirmed by the image of Nebuchadnezzar. This would give support to the idea that Yeshua also ministered for 7 years in His earthly body. This idea gives rise to the idea that the Anti-Christ will not truly come to power until the beginning of the Tribulation but if this is the beginning of the Tribulation, then he should have the power to rule and this seal does not verify that rule over the earth as of yet.

Common Theories about the Anti-Christ:

Anti-Christ is a system of world domination.

Anti-Christ is a physical person who will miss-lead and deceive the elect into thinking he is the Messiah.

Man, of Sin: 2 Thessalonians 2

Son of perdition: Revelation 8-12, Daniel 8:24

He will exalt himself.

Will accept being worshipped as if he is Elohim.

He is the "Little Horn" of Daniel 7;

Prince who shall come: Daniel 9

Willful King: Daniel 11

He is not a "religious system or economic system" as he comes from the pit in the end of days. A system cannot come from the pit.

Anti-Christ is a person, the resurrected Judas Iscariot. It is proposed here that the anti-Christ is none other than the resurrected Judas Iscariot *who went to his own place in perdition* and comes forth from perdition to fulfill his role in the last days. In Revelations, it was stated that the "anti-Christ *was (that is he existed before the time of John's writing), but is not (he is no longer on earth at the time of John's writing), but will be (resurrected from perdition)."* Both Judas and the Anti-Christ are referred to as the *son of perdition.*

He will be of Jewish descent: if another (the Antichrist) comes in his own name, him (the Antichrist, a person) you will receive". John 5: 39-43.

He will not regard the God of his fathers (Jewish fathers). Daniel 11:37

The Antichrist will engineer a peace-pact between Israel (Judaism) and the Arab world (Islam) because of a war that started between Abraham's sons, Isaac and Ishmael about 4,000 years ago (Gen 21). The offspring of Abraham still despise each other, and the intensity is growing and will continue to grow.

It is evident that this is not Satan. Satan is in heaven (and earth) too and will be cast out of heaven later. This power could be the intended message of the rider of the white horse, a ruler\king coming to conquer, but not yet having the means to do so (lack of arrows) or according to Ezekiel, who lost his power (lost his arrows).

In Daniel, this king, if it is the anti-Christ, will uproot 3 of the 10 horns of the last beast. He is the "little horn" in 2 different visions of Daniel.

It is a mistake to believe that the Anti-Christ will come by force. He will come by flatteries and political strategies. Daniel 11:23 tells us he will work "deceitfully". He will allow the Temple to be rebuilt on Mount Moriah. The Muslims also believe in the return of the Messiah, only just not OUR Messiah. This is why they will allow the rebuilding of the Temple.

(Quran) "When Jesus came with clear proofs (of Allah's Sovereignty), he said: I have come unto you with wisdom, and to make plain some of that concerning which ye differ. So, keep your duty to Allah, and obey me. Lo! Allah, He is my Lord and your Lord. So, worship Him. This is a right path. But the factions among them differed. Then woe unto those who do wrong from the doom of a painful day. Await they aught save the Hour that it shall come upon them suddenly, when they know not? Friends on that day will be foes one to another, save those who kept their duty (to Allah)." Qur'an sura 43 (az-Zukhruf), ayah 57-67.

The Anti-Christ will come from the Tribe of Judah. The Antichrist becomes sole ruler and military dictator. He controls a *cashless* economy by means of computerized 666-related body marks. A cashless society is already being pushed forward by the WEF (headed by Klaus Schwab). He lives in two time periods: He was, but is not (at the time of John), but will be.

- **Middle East Situation (1988-1994 CE):** The Israelis assassinate the Jihad leader. At this time, a battle in Jordon causes Jordon to give up the entire West Bank to Israel. Intifada is created to support Arafat in his war against the Jews. The PLO gets embassy status with all the Arab nations. The PLO no longer bothers to deny terrorist activities against the Jews. The following year, Arafat is elected as president of the PLO. Jordon erupts into civil wars and riots between Muslims and Christians. Lebanon and Israel increase cross the border fire. Much of the fighting breaks out between Muslim factions.

Sadam Hussein gained control over Iraq (1990) and is building what he refers to as the New Babylonian Empire. He threatens Israel with nerve gas and with mass destruction. Hussein had the bow, the nuclear weapons, but he was not able to use them. He had no arrows as they were taken away from him (Ezekiel). In further actions, he threatens the other Arabic nations unless they reduce oil production, hoping to put the world into an oil shortage.

The U.S. and Britain send ships to the Persian Gulf as a result and invade Kuwait, which has been taken over by Hussein. The war erupts over Kuwait and the oil there. The invasion of the U.S. causes the other Arabic nations alarm and they turn against Hussein. Most of Hussein's troops surrendered willingly without a fight on the land attacks.

Top officials of the PLO are assassinated and Arafat blames Israel. The faction of Nidal in Iraq takes responsibility, leaving Israel innocent. Arafat has sided with Hussein and invites a war with the U.S. Iraq attacks Israel with missiles, but it is the U.S. who retaliates with further destruction of Baghdad. The city is devastated by U.S. missiles (but not destroyed).

Around 1989, America (CIA) began training the Mujahedin in Afghanistan. This resulted in the Al Qaeda, the largest terrorist group on the world. In 1990-1991, the Persian Gulf War started which resulted in Hussein being expelled as dictator.

- **United States Situation (1988-1994 CE):** On September 21, 1989, the courts deliberated about making abortion illegal, but they reversed their decision and left it alone. The very next day, hurricane Hugo destroyed Charleston South Carolina. McTernan believes that the 2 events are directly related and shows the disfavor of America's decisions in HaShem's eyes. McTerman (see Bibliography) puts together major catastrophes with news of decisions that go against HaShem. He makes a good case that HaShem doesn't wait long before these bad decisions resulting in floods, tornados, earthquakes, and hurricanes. HaShem is trying to get our attention, but He even said through Isaiah that "listening, they didn't hear".

A pro-abortion rally is quickly followed by a hurricane that does over 1 billion dollars in damage in North Carolina. An anti-Israel speech by George Bush leads to another huge storm in New England. This was later referred to as the *Perfect Storm*. McTernan places the events side by side in "*USA Today*". In the following year, a pro-abortion rally leveled against the Christian organization called *Operation Rescue* is followed by another 7.1 earthquake in southern California. During the rally, the group was openly blasphemous against HaShem. Soon after, the Rodney King trials led to riots in Los Angeles. Another gay pride rally was quickly followed by another earthquake measured at 7.6. McTernan reports that this earthquake was different from all other earthquakes in that it didn't follow a fault line. This same year, 1992, Bush makes another anti-Israel speech which is followed by Hurricane Andrew which did over 30 billion dollars in damage and left 180,000 homeless.

In Texas, prayer in schools was banned. This news article was next to another article where a tornado devastated Fort Worth Texas. In a meeting between President Clinton and Barak of Israel, there were talks about giving up some land in Israel. This led to the stock market dropping 600 points at a time when no drop was expected and in Israel, the government collapsed leaving no government for a time. McTernan puts enough of these headlines together with matching catastrophes to rule out "coincidence".

George W Bush (Sr.) became president in 1989. He was responsible for encouraging Israel to "give up" some of their land: "One of the most controversial moments of his single-term presidency was when Bush delayed Israel loan guarantees until it halted its settlement building in the West Bank and Gaza and entered a peace conference with the Palestinians, what would later become known as the Madrid Peace Conference. (*Times of Israel*)"

- **Russia:** Russian is on the verge of collapse as communism fails to keep them financially secure. Russia loses considerable power in the *Cold War.* East and West Germany re-unite and the wall between them is torn down. The next year, Gorbachev is ousted and the Soviet Union collapses.

- **Second Seal: (KJ-Revelation)** "{6:3} and when he had opened the second seal, I heard the second beast say, Come and see. {6:4} and there went out another horse [that was] red: and [power] was given to him that sat thereon to take peace from the earth, and that *they should kill one another.* and there was given unto him a great sword."

The four beasts are part of the first four seals to be opened. It might be assumed that the order of the beasts corresponds to the order given: And the first being is like a lion, and the second being like an ox, and the third being has a human face, and the fourth being is like an eagle in flight. This second beast would be the ox, a symbol of sacrifice (as in the burnt offering). The results of this rider were that he brought war but he did not kill.

(LXXNT-Revelation) "³ and when the Lamb opened the second seal, I heard the voice of the second (living being) being saying, "Come." ⁴and another horse came, a red one, and the one sitting on it, to him *the order* was given to take peace away from the earth, that is, so that they slaughter one another. And to him was given a large sword." This taking away of peace didn't come from the first rider. This rider brings war among the nations.

(MTJ-Revelation) "|3| and when he opened the chotam hasheyni ("second seal"), I heard hasheniyah of HaChayyot ("the second of the living beings") saying, "Come and see! |4| and another sus ("horse") went forth, a flame-red one, and to the one sitting on it was given him to take shalom from ha'aretz ("the earth") with men slaughtering one another, and was given to him a cherev gedolah ("great sword"). [ZECHARYAH 1:8; 6:2]". This horse was "flame red", something not brought out in the KJ or LXXNT.

(KJ - Matthew 24) "{24:6} and ye shall hear of wars and rumors of wars: see that ye be not troubled: for all [these things] must come to pass, but the end is not yet. {24:7} for nation shall rise against nation, and kingdom against kingdom: and there shall be famines, and pestilences, and earthquakes, in diver's places."

This supports Theory 2 that the opening of the scroll seals takes 49 years "but the end is not yet". Matthew indicates that wars and rumors of wars take place, but the "end is not yet".

(KJ - Luke 21) "{21:9} but when ye shall hear of wars and commotions, be not terrified: for these things must first come to pass; but the end [is] not by and by. {21:10} then said he unto them,

Nation shall rise against nation, and kingdom against kingdom: {21:11} and great earthquakes shall be in diver's places, and famines, and pestilences; and fearful sights and great signs shall there be from heaven."

(KJ - Zechariah 1) "{1:8} I saw by night, and behold a man riding upon a red horse, and he stood among the myrtle trees that [were] in the bottom; and behind him [were there] red horses, speckled, and white. {1:9} then said I, O my lord, what [are] these? And the angel that talked with me said unto me, I will shew thee what these [be.] {1:10} and the man that stood among the myrtle trees answered and said, these [are they] whom the LORD hath sent to walk to and fro through the earth. {1:11} And they answered the angel of the LORD that stood among the myrtle trees, and said, we have walked to and fro through the earth, and, behold, *all the earth sits still, and is at rest.*"

Wars and rumors of wars. This is the time when the wars start taking place around the world. The Middle East is a cauldron of issues between the Arabs and the Israelites. Russia and the U.S. are still in a cold war.

Between 2000 and 2018 more than 3911 major earthquakes have happened. This is far more than the number of earthquakes in the years of 1900 to 1918. This is more than a 2000% increase in earthquakes in a hundred years.

This rider carries a sword and instead of destroying, he incites the nations to destroy each other. This isn't necessarily by war. With the changes in handling of food, the World Order seeks to starve populations to decrease the growing populations. Peace is not necessarily taken by war, but by subtle schemes against one another. This rider is announced by the second living being, but we are not told which one.

Dates according to Theory 2: Yovel End of Days: 5958 - 5964 AT by MT

7382 - 7388 AT by LXX;

1995 - 2001 CE by estimated Julian

Progression of the Riders on the Red Horses: In the time of Zachariah, the rider of the red horse was said to report that peace was in the land. This was during the time of the rebuilding of the Temple in Jerusalem. There was no war around Jerusalem. The rider of the red horse is now able to remove peace from the land, a reversal of Zachariah. Jerusalem is at the center of the wars at the end of days. This progression affects Jerusalem.

(Luke) {21:20} and when ye shall see Jerusalem compassed with armies, then know that the desolation thereof is nigh."

This rider had the designation to "take peace" from the land of Israel.

- **World Events:** The U.S. and Britain bomb Iraq with a new uprising of Hussein. During this year, Secretary of State Albright determined that Israel should give up 13 percent of its land. This was followed by a huge hurricane that slammed the coast. Israel supported the notion. This decision was followed 6 days later by tornadoes in San Antonio and declared San Antonio a disaster area from tornadoes.

  The European Union approves radioactive treatment of foods (which supports the idea that the peace that is removed by subtle means). This kills the germs, but the side effect is that it also kills the nutrition, leaving the food as useless for nutritional purposes. "Nexus Magazine" reports that the purpose of this was for future use in genocide cases where populations could be slowly starved to death for crowd and population control. Over 1 fourth of the population worldwide is reported to be starving or malnourished. During this time, President Bush signs an agreement with the Worldwide FDA to allow radiation treatment of food which removes bacteria and all nutritional value of the foods.

  Osama ben Laden (or someone) attacks the Twin Towers and starts a terrorist attack against the U.S. This allows Bush to sign in bills that are aimed at controlling terrorism in the U.S., but ultimately takes away much of the freedom and rights of Americans. In his actions, military control over the U.S. will be allowed at the discretion of the government. Anyone can be investigated for violations of terrorism at the discretion of the government. Bush instigates using police agencies (CIA, FBI, etc) for political purposes, allowing corruption to infiltrate the agencies

  Israel and the PLO increase attacks against one another as well. The following year, Israel manages to capture Arafat and places him on house arrest. The Taliban becomes the main Islamic radical factions to terrorize the world in individual actions. They attack Buddhist temples in Afghanistan. Two years later, the U.S. and Britain capture Saddam Hussein and topple the Hussein Empire.

- **Little Horn:** Greece becomes the twelfth nation to join the European Union. This officially restores Greece as one of the final 10 nations of the image of Nebuchadnezzar. The vision of Daniel about Greece indicates that Greece, Egypt, and Syria (all one of the 4 kingdoms of the Greek Empire of

Alexander) will be restored in the end times. This is already true about Greece and Egypt. Syria is part of the Babylonian Empire. The "little horn" of Daniel is said to derive from the Greek Empire of Alexander the Great.

- **False Prophet**: The Anti-Christ and the False Prophet (antithesis of John the Baptist) will attempt to anti-copy the ministry of Yeshua. This is the reason for the 7-year Tribulation as its anti-copies the ministry of Yeshua (adding support to a 7-year ministry of Yeshua). With this belief comes the idea that the False Prophet will be about 30 years old when he starts this ministry in 2030 in imitation of Christ at the beginning of the ministry of Christ. This leads us the year of his birth to be the year 2000 CE. (This cannot be validated but is surmised as what might have happened).

Many Christians believed that this year would be the year of His coming, because of the millennium change to 2000. The problem is that the calendar is not correctly matched with Biblical time and ultimately, all of this is pure conjecture. None of this can be validated and won't be known until "after the fact".

- **Anti-Christ**: (LXXTR-I John 2) "$^{22}$Who is the liar, if not someone denying as follows, "Jesus is not the Anointed One"? This is antichrist, someone denying the Father and the Son. $^{23}$Everyone who denies the Son, does not have the Father either. Someone who confesses the Son, has the Father as well."

Many interpreters believe that the Anti-Christ and False Prophet are systems, rather than people. It is suggested here that the Anti-Christ (a person, not a system) is going to be that of the resurrected Judas Iscariot who went to his own place when he hung himself and comes out of the Abyss where he went to his own place. A resurrection does not imply birth. John indicates that the Anti-Christ was, is not, and will be again. At the time of John's vision, the Anti-Christ had already been on the earth once, as he *was, but is not at the time of John.* The only person that fits that is Judas Iscariot, called the Son of Perdition. The Anti-Christ is also referred to by that title.

**Third Seal:** (KJ-Revelation) "{6:5} and when he had opened the third seal, I heard the third beast say ("human face"), Come and see. And I beheld, and lo a black horse; and he that sat on him had a pair of balances in his hand. {6:6} And I heard a voice in the midst of the four beasts say, A measure of wheat for a penny, and three measures of barley for a penny; and [see] thou hurt not the oil and the wine."

The seals might not be limited to "their" week, but may extend throughout the length of the following seals. Seal 3 is an example: This seal is telling us that the price of food will skyrocket and a day's food will cost most of "a day's pay". While this was strong during this week of years, it did not necessarily "end" with this same week.

Oil and wine are foods of the wealthy. Famine and disease have extended past this seal. With theory 1, this presents no problem as the entire opening of all the seals takes place in 7 years. With the Yovel theory, this presents no problem but the effects of the famine and disease extends through more than 7 years. In 2021 AD, a worldwide disease (Covid) was responsible for millions of deaths (either directly or through bad vaccines distributed).

(LXXNT-Revelation) "[5] and when the third seal was opened, I heard the voice of the third being saying, "Come." And I looked, and behold, a black horse, and the one sitting on it holding a pair of scales in his hands. [6] And I heard a voice as if in the midst of the four living beings, saying, "A quart of wheat for a day's wage, or three barley loaves for a day's wage. And don't you damage the oil or wine." To damage the oil or wine, one has to damage the source fruit. Wine cannot be bruised, and olive oil can only go bad if exposed to sun light for extended periods of time. Damaged wine or oil is useless to the body so the foods go to waste.

(MTJ-Revelation) "|5| and when he opened the chotam hashlishi (" third seal"), I heard hashlishit of HaChayyot (the third of the living beings), saying, "Come and see! And I saw and Hinei, a sus shakhor ("black horse"), and the one sitting on it having a pair of scales in his yad (hand). [ZECHARYAH 6:2] |6| And I heard, as it were, a kol (voice) in the midst of the Arbah Chayyot (four living beings), saying, "A quart of wheat for a denarius and shloshah quarts of barley for a denarius, but the shemen (oil) and the yayin (wine) you may not harm." [Ezekiel 4:16]

(LXXTR-Ezekiel) "4:16 Moreover he said to me, Son of man, behold, I will break the staff of bread in Jerusalem: and they shall eat bread by weight, and with fearfulness; and they shall drink water by measure, and in dismay: 4:17 that they may want bread and water, and be dismayed one with another, and pine away in their iniquity."

In Zechariah 6:6, the black horses drawing the chariot go into the north with the white horse chariot following the black. These are horses pulling chariots and not the same as the horses in the seal. If the Tribulation has started, believers are not spared and they have not been taken away off the earth yet. The rider of this black horse has nothing to do with conquering or war, but famine and disease.

The price of food is reported by the rider of this black horse to be extravagantly priced, costing a day's wages for a day's supply of food.

There is a progression of the color of the horses: White; Flaming Red; Black. The white horse came to lead into conquering. The red horse takes away peace. Now, this black horse attacks the population by attacking the goods that the population needs to live. The last horse is green and represents death.

In the Yovel interpretation, this rider takes a week of years.

Dates for Theory 2 (Yovel Interpretation): 5965 - 5971 A.T. by MT

7389 - 7395 A.T. by LXX;

2002 - 2008 C.E. By Julian:

- **World:** "US News Today, March 2008" reports that due to the energy crisis, many foods are being used for fuel. This causes a food shortage that leads to the rising cost of foods. This leads to the fact that across the world, *the average price of food for a day is equal to the average daily wage for a day* reported in US News. This directly verifies the results of the third seal. The resulting famine will be a longer-term event, verifying that the seals are not limited to a week of years, a single year, or a few months. Over the time of this seal, the prices of food will raise into unexpected levels. Over the next few years, America is hit with huge economic losses, resulting in thousands of jobs and homes lost. Unemployment will reach the highest level since the Depression of the late 1930's. Worldwide famine will destroy millions of lives.

Africa and India are hit with major famines and starvation. Charities are formed to send food to the starving children in Africa. Famine was reported to threaten more than 15 million in 2002. In Niger and Guatemala, children were dying of hunger by the millions.

Inflation rose averaged from 1.6 to 3.8 over the years 2000 to 2008 CE. In 2022, inflation reached an average of 8.0 over the entire year.

New Orleans is wiped out by Hurricane Katrina, leaving thousands homeless, killing thousands more. Hurricane Katrina was a devastating Category 5 Atlantic hurricane that caused 1,836 fatalities and damage estimated between $97.4 billion to $145.5 billion in late August 2005, particularly in the city of New Orleans and its surrounding area.

- **Anti-God Sentiment:** The growing movements against HaShem become numerous. Satanism and Atheism permeates the schools, as the teachings of Evolutionary scientists tries to wipe out HaShem as the creator of the heavens and the earth. The rise of the "New Atheism", a label that has been applied, sometimes pejoratively, to outspoken critics of theism and religion, prompted by a series of essays published in late 2006, including *The God Delusion, Breaking the Spell, God Is Not Great, The End of Faith,* and *Letter to a Christian Nation.* Richard Dawkins also propounds a more visible form of atheist activism which he light-heartedly describes as "militant atheism ".

- **Fourth Seal: (KJ-Revelation)** "{6:7} and when he had opened the fourth seal, I heard the voice of the fourth beast ("flying eagle") say, Come and see. {6:8} and I looked, and behold a pale horse: and his name that sat on him was Death, and Hell followed with him. And power was given unto them over the fourth part of the earth, to kill with sword, and with hunger, and with death, and with the beasts of the earth."

(LXXNT-Revelation) "7 and when the fourth seal was opened, I heard the voice of the fourth being saying, "Come." 8 And I looked, and behold, a pale green horse, and the one who is sitting on (The preposition "on" is different with this rider than the first three. When you read this version of the prepositional phrase out loud, this one has a more grave sound to it. It is longer and more spelled out) it, his name is Death, and Hades is trailing after him ("is following after him"); and authority is given them (to them) over one fourth of the earth, to kill them with war, and famine, and death, and by the wild animals of the earth."

The word "pale" is translated from the Greek word "chloros" that actually means green. "Chloros" appears four times in the Brit Chadashah. Three times it is translated as "green". Only Revelation 6: 8 translates it as "pale". The English word "chlorophyll" comes from this Greek word.

(LV-Revelation) "And behold a pale horse: and he that sat upon him, his name was Death. And hell followed him. And power was given to him over the four parts of the earth, to kill with sword, with famine and with death and with the beasts of the earth."

(MTJ-Revelation) "|7| and when he opened the chotam harevi'i ("the fourth seal"), I heard the kol (voice) of hareve'it ("the fourth") of HaChayyot ("the living beings") saying, "Come and see! |8| And I saw, and, Hinei, a sus yerakrak ("a greenish pale horse"), and the one sitting upon ("epano-upon, over", STRG1883, - this is different than the other 3 riders who sat "on" is STRG1909 or "epi") it, that rider's name was Mavet ("Thanatos-death", STRG2288), and She'ol ("Hades-grave, hell", STRG86) was following with him. And there was given to them samchut (authority) over a quarter of ha'aretz ("the earth"), to kill with cherev ("sword") and with ra'av ("famine") and with mavet ("death") and by the chayyot ("beasts") of ha'aretz ("the earth"). [ZECHARYAH 6:3; HOSHEA 13:14; YIRMEYAH 15:2, 3; 24:10; YECHEZKEL 5:12, 17]"

(KJ-Matthew) "{24:7} for nation shall rise against nation, and kingdom against kingdom: and there shall be famines, and pestilences, and earthquakes, in diver's places. {24:8} all these [are] the beginning of sorrows."

There is a progression of the color of the horses: White; Flaming Red; Black. The white horse came to lead into conquering. The red horse takes away peace. The black horse attacks the population by attacking the goods that the population needs to live; famine and disease. This last horse is pale or green and represents death.

In 1956 only 46 million people died. The voice was that of the fourth living creature (flying eagle). Death was followed by Hades for those who fall to the green pale horse. They will be judged to eternal hell. There are about 8 billion people world-wide. This could be connected to the result of seal 3 which allowed famine and disease to increase. The death "rate" is not the actual death count. For instance:

2009: 54 million

2010: 54 million

2011: 54 million

2012: 55 million

2013: 55 million

2014: 55 million

2015: 56 million

Total over 7 years: 383 million is equal to almost one fourth of the population.

The population in 2013 is 2 billion people.

"And power was given unto them over the fourth part of the earth, to kill with sword, and with hunger, and with death"

Date for this week of years: 5972 – 5978 A.T. by MT

7396 – 7402 A.T. by LXX;

2009 – 2015 C.E. By Julian

- **Increase of Death:** After 2007, the death rate in America took a major uphill climb where before 2002, the death rate was fairly level compared to the population growth. Violent crimes increased. The growing number of illegal immigrants are slipping into America. Mexico is growing more and more unstable as the Drug Cartels gain control of the country and the government. Citizens try to escape the violence growing there and go to a more prosperous country. The current population approaches a level of unrest over the care of the immigrants escaping from the violence of South America and Mexico.

In Africa, internal wars between religious factions increase killing thousands. Smaller villages were overrun with new "tyrants" and dictators.

Since the increased deaths applies mainly to non-believers of Christ, the deaths are followed by Hades or Hell. These people will die outside of the protection of our Savior and Lord.

- **Fifth Seal:** (KJ-Revelation) "{6:9} and when he had opened the fifth seal, I saw *under the altar* the souls of them that were slain for the word of God, and for the testimony which they held: {6:10} And they cried with a loud voice, saying, How long, O Lord, holy and true, dost thou not judge and avenge our blood on them that dwell on the earth? {6:11} And white robes were given unto every one of them; and it was said unto them, that *they should rest yet for a little season*, until their fellow servants also and their brethren, that should be killed as they [were,] should be fulfilled."

"Rest" is "anapauo" in Greek, which is from "ana"- up, and "pauo"-to make to cease. The word describes a cessation from toil, refreshment, and an intermission (STRG373). Although they "rest", they are also crying; they are not in an unconscious state as some denominations teaching – that all Believers sleep until resurrection day. Samuel did cry to Saul for "waking him from his sleep" by the Witch of Endor. These souls are told to "rest a little longer". The souls of the unredeemed are in Hades; which is not a place of rest, but of torment (Luke 16: 23).

(LXXNT-Revelation) "[9] and when the fifth seal was opened, I saw beneath the altar, the souls of those slain for the word of God and for the witness (of the lamb) that they were bearing. [10] and they cried out with a loud voice, saying, "Until when, O Master, holy and true, are you refraining from adjudicating and avenging our blood from those who dwell on the earth?" [11] and they were given each a white robe, and it was prescribed for them that they would take rest a little while longer, until the number of their fellow-servants and brethren was also complete, those about to be killed even as they."

(LXXTR-Revelation) "9 And when the fifth seal was opened, I saw beneath the altar, the souls of those slain for the word of God and for the witness that they were bearing. 10 And they were crying out with a loud voice, saying, "Until when, O Master, holy and true, are you refraining from adjudicating and avenging our blood from those who dwell on the earth?" 11 And white robes were given to each one of them, and it was prescribed for them that they would take rest a little while longer, until such time the number of their fellow-servants and brethren would also be complete, those about to be killed even as they."

(MTJ) "|9| and when he opened the chotam hachamishi ("fifth seal"), I saw underneath the

Mizbe'ach ("altar") the nefashot ("souls") of the ones having died al Kiddush ha-Shem, having been slain as martyrs because of the dvar Hashem ("Word of G-d") and because of their solemn eidus ("testimony") which they had given. [SHEMOT 29:12; VAYIKRA 4:7] |10| and they cried out, saying, Rabbono shel Olam, HaKadosh and HaNe'eman, ad mosai ("how much longer") is it to be until you judge and avenge dahmeinu ("our blood") on the inhabitants of ha'aretz ("the earth")? [Psalms 119:84; ZECHARYAH 1:12

(KJ-Zechariah) "{1:12} Then the angel of the LORD answered and said, O LORD of hosts, how long wilt thou not have mercy on Jerusalem and on the cities of Judah, against which thou hast had indignation these threescore and ten years?"; DEVARIM 32:43; MELACHIM BAIS 9:7; TEHILLIM 79:10] |11| And they were each given a kittel (white robe) and it was told them that they will rest yet a little while ("chronos - time(s), plural indicating a season", STRG5550), until the mispar ("number") should be complete of their fellow avadim ("servants") and their Achim b'Moshiach, the ones about to die al kiddush ha- Shem, being about to be killed as martyrs as they were."

(KJ – Matthew 24) "{24:9} Then shall they deliver you up to be afflicted, and shall kill you: and ye shall be hated of all nations for my name's sake. {24:10} and then shall many be offended, and shall betray one another, and shall hate one another. {24:11} and many false prophets shall rise, and shall deceive many."

(LV) "And it was said to them that they should rest for a little time(s) till their fellow servants and their brethren, who are to be slain even as they, should be filled up."

These souls were not sleeping in death, but were kept "under the altar". Their voices were hears. These were the ones still "resting", meaning they had not yet been resurrected in the Rapture from the ground yet. The number of martyrs was not yet fulfilled.

The 4 living creatures have spoken about the 4 horsemen. They spoke no longer. The word for times, "Chronos", is plural and the word for times in Daniel refers to years. It doesn't say how many, as in Daniel it says times (2 years), time (1 year), and half year (6 months). If this "little time" applies, it could mean a number of month or years.

By the 7-year interpretation this can only mean months, but by the Yovel interpretation of the Seals of the Scroll, this might mean as many 14 years, up to the opening of seal 7.

Seals 1 to 4 are on the "inside" of the scroll. Seals 5 to 7 are on the outside.

There are 2 altars in heaven: The Brazen Altar and Altar of Sacrifice (Burnt offerings).

Date of Yovel interpretation: 5979 – 5985 A.T. by MT;

7403 – 7409 A.T. by LXX;

2016 – 2022 C.E. By Julian

- **World Persecutions**: In Africa, several days of news reported up to 1500 Christians were beheaded by Muslim factions in Africa. Not just one day, but over many days this took place. BBC news reported on the beheadings, publicized by the Muslim factions. In Egypt, Christians are tortured and imprisoned for their beliefs. Believers will be persecuted to extreme levels! Believers include both Christians who do not conform to the worldwide church and to Jews who have seen the error of their ways and accepted Yeshua as the Messiah. This news is not future tense, but happening at the time of this writing.

Strangely, this level of persecution is not seen in the U.S. which is a bad sign in that the persecutions take place where Christians and churches are more loyal to the Word of God and to the Savior. This gives us a bad taste in that while there are many preachers on cable and TV, they do not seem to be "true faithers in Christ", but corrupt men seeking riches and fame. Satan has nothing to worry about with these men, so the persecutions of these "false believers" is not important enough to martyr.

There are some of these false Christians who "testify" of persecutions mainly because they are being taunted and rejected by modern secularists in science, schools, and government. Death escapes these men except where Hashem chooses for a few to die by disease or old age.

**Israel:** By midway of the year 2018 CE, Israel will have approximately 98-99 percent of the world Jewish population within its borders. The year, 2018 CE, marks 70 years since Israel became a nation, which is the reverse of the exile of Judah, (not Jerusalem). "Isaiah 43:5 *I will bring your children from the east, I will gather you from the west, I will say to the north "Give them up", and to the south, "Do not hold them back." Bring my sons from afar and my daughters from the ends of the earth. The days are coming when I will bring my people Israel and Judah back from captivity and restore them to the land. After I have sent them away, I will gather you from the nations and give you back the land of Israel."*

Ezekiel 38:1 the prophecy of Ezekiel against Gog and Magog. I have called you into arms and in future years you will invade a land recovered from war. They had been brought out from the nations and now live in safety. You will advance like a storm. You will devise a scheme and will attack a peaceful unsuspecting people. In that day, you will come from your place in the far north and many nations with you. I will bring you against my land. At that time, there will be a great earthquake in Israel. The mountains will be overturned and every wall will crumble. Every man's sword will be against his brother and I will pour down torrents of rain, hailstones, and burning sulfur. I will bring you from the far north against the mountains of Israel and on the mountains of Israel, you will fall. I will give you as food to all kinds of carrion. I will send fire on Magog and those living in safety in the coastlands. Then those who live in Israel will use the weapons for fuel for 7 years, in the Valley of Hamon Gog (Hordes of Gog). For 7 months, Israel will bury the dead and men will be employed to clean the land. Every kind of bird will feed there."

- **State of the World:** Violence in the U.S. grows to unprecedented levels. Rapes, murders abound in the major cities of Chicago, New York, Baltimore, Los Angeles, and San Francisco, as well in major cities in Europe. While the leftist radicals seek to take away guns from the common citizen, leaving them defenseless against the growing criminal gangs. Leftist government tends to give way to the growing criminal elements and even protect the "poor criminals" from prosecution. Other countries see a large increase in criminal activity. Sex trafficking becomes a common theme as little children are included as victims. Children are exposed and groomed to be victims of sexual predators.

A new phenomenon in Hollywood is about the fact that when children are terrified, they produce a hormone that is believed to extend life to adults. The Hollywood elite have formed secret societies where children are kidnapped and terrorized to create this hormone. The number of missing children has grown exponentially in the past decade.

- **Progression of Seals compared to Events of Crucifixion:** There appears to be a direct connection between the events of the Crucifixion and the Opening of the Seals by the Lamb. The Crucifixion was all about Christ at the center of history and now it is Christ alone who can reverse His crucifixion by opening the Seals of the Scroll. This may seem to be a stretch for some, but relating the following events has some validity.

    c. Seal 1: Judas betrays Christ is related to the first Rider to conquer but he cannot complete his conquering. He has the "bow", the 30 pieces of silver, but he cannot complete his transaction.
    d. Seal 2: Peace removed from land is related to Christ obtains peace for what's coming in Garden
    e. Seal 3: Famine and Disease as False Trial by Jews brings about the declaration of death by trial by the Jews.
    f. Seal 4: Death and Disease continue as the trial by Pontus Pilate seals the fate of Christ.
    g. Seal 5: The martyrs must wait a bit as Christ is crucified, the first martyr.

    h. Seal 6: Darkness covers the land as Christ hangs on the cross.
    i. Huge earthquake between seal 6 and 7 is related to the earthquake at death of Christ.
    j. Seal 7: Satan is cast out of heaven is related to Yeshua being sent to Hades.

Harvest of angels for resurrection of the saints is related to the First Resurrection of Christ

- **Sixth Seal:** (KJ-Revelation) "{6:12} and I beheld when he had opened the sixth seal, and, lo, there was a great earthquake; and the sun became black as sackcloth of hair, and the moon became as blood; {6:13} And the stars of heaven fell unto the earth, even as a fig tree casts her untimely figs, when she is shaken of a mighty wind. {6:14} and the heaven departed as a scroll when it is rolled together; and every mountain and island were moved out of their places. {6:15} and the kings of the earth, and the great men, and the rich men, and the chief captains, and the mighty men, and every bondman, and every free man, hid themselves in the dens and in the rocks of the mountains; {6:16} And said to the mountains and rocks, Fall on us, and hide us from the face of him that sits on the throne, and from the wrath of the Lamb: {6:17} For the great day of his wrath is come; and who shall be able to stand?"

    (LXXNT-Revelation) "[12]And I watched as he opened the sixth seal, and a mighty earthquake took place, and the sun became black like animal hair sack-cloth, and the full moon became like blood, [13] and the stars of heaven fell to the earth, as a fig tree shaken by a strong wind casts its unripe figs, [14] and the sky retreated like a scroll being rolled up, and every mountain and island was removed from its place. [15] And the kings of the earth, and the great and the generals and the rich and the powerful, and everyone, slave and free, hid themselves in caverns, and among the rocks of the mountains, [16] and they are saying to the mountains and to the rocks, "Fall on us, and hide us from the face of the One sitting on the throne, and from the wrath of the Lamb; [17] for the great day of their wrath has come, and who will be able to stand?"

    (MTJ-Revelation) "|12| And I saw when he opened the chotam hashish ("sixth seal"), a great earthquake occurred and the shemesh ("sun") became shakhor ("black") as sackcloth made of hair and the whole levanah ("moon") became like dahm. [Psalms 97:4; Isaiah 29:6; Ezekiel 38:19; Isaiah 50:3] |13| and the kokhavim ("stars") of Shomayim fell to ha'aretz (the earth), as an etz te'enah ("fig tree") casts off its unripe figs when being shaken by a great wind. [YESHAYAH 34:4] |14| And Shomayim split apart as a megillah scroll being rolled up; and every mountain and island were moved out of their places. [TEHILLIM 46:2; YESHAYAH 54:10; YIRMEYAH 4:24; YECHEZKEL 38:20; NACHUM 1:5] |15| And the melachim ("kings") of ha'aretz ("the earth") and the gedolim ("great ones") and the military leaders and the oishirim ("rich men") and the strong men and all avadim ("slaves") and Bnei Chorin ("freedmen") hid themselves in the caves and in the rocks of the mountains. [YESHAYAH 2:10, 19, 21] |16| and they say to the mountains and to the rocks, fall on us and hide us from the face of the One sitting on the Kes ("Throne") and from the za'am ("wrath, anger", 16:1f) of the SEH ("Lamb", *SHEMOT 12:3; YESHAYAH 53:7 Moshiach*), [HOSHEA 10:8] |17| because the Yom HaGadol, the Yom HaZa'am, the Great Day of Their Wrath has come, and who is able to stand? [Joel 1:15; 2:1, 2, 11, 31; Zephaniah 1:14, 15; Nahum 1:6; Malachi 3:2]"

(KJ- Joel 2:31) "{2:31} the sun shall be turned into darkness, and the moon into blood, *before* the great and the terrible day of the LORD come."

When this happens, we know that the great and terrible day of the Lord is near.

(Luke) "{21:25} and there shall be signs in the sun, and in the moon, and in the stars; and upon the earth distress of nations, with perplexity; the sea and the waves roaring. {21:26} Men's hearts failing them for fear, and for looking after those things which are coming on the earth: for the powers of heaven shall be shaken."

For the 1 week of year's interpretation of Revelation, it is unknown where this falls in the chronology. Still to happen is the casting out of Satan from heaven, but many believe that Revelation goes "back in time" for this to occur. This is the last week of years before the Tribulation according to the Yovel interpretation of the 7 seals. According to the traditional interpretation, this must take place in or around year 3 of the Tribulation before the final seal which holds the 7 trumpets and the vials. The Days of Wrath of HaShem could refer to the coming "trumpets and vials" of seal 7. Besides the earthquake and signs in heaven, nothing seems to happen on earth with this seal.

In the Yovel interpretation, this week period of 7 years (of the seal number 6) shall show us many signs in heaven and many asteroids and meteorites falling to earth in great proportions. The earth will be beaten and battered by the signs in heaven. In this interpretation, Satan is not due to be cast out for another 3-6 years. The six years seem to pass without any catastrophes on earth, only in heaven.

There is no sign that the events of this seal have taken place. An earthquake of large proportions is mentioned here, but this earthquake seems to be just one of many taking place at this time. This seal seems to separate seals 6 and 7 from seals 1 to 5. The Days of Wrath of HaShem begin with this seal.

Date for Yovel interpretation: 5986 – 5992 A.T. by MT;

7410 – 7416 A.T. by LXX;

2023 – 2929 C.E. By Julian (?).

- **Earthquake:** Sometime within the opening of seal 6 a large earthquake or many large earthquakes are due to hit. The stars fell from the sky indicates a huge meteor shower hitting the earth. In December 2023, many meteorite showers appear that are visible to the naked eye. The mountains and islands were moved out of their place. This is similar event is reported to have occurred during the time of the Exodus. The Aztecs and Incas record that when they woke up in the morning some mountains had disappeared, and new ones had appeared (Popol Vul).

There is a possibility that the earth and moon will be restored to their former estate around the sun, returning to a 360-day year. The famine and wars will continue from earlier seals.

During this time, the killing of "true believers" continues to add to the numbers of martyrs. There is nothing as of yet to indicate a rapture has or takes place during this period of time.

A large earthquake hit turkey near the town of Gaziantep, was closely followed by numerous aftershocks - including one quake which was almost as large as the first. The first earthquake was big - it registered as 7.8, classified as "major" on the official magnitude scale. It broke along about 100km (62 miles) of fault line, causing serious damage to buildings near the fault. Prof Joanna Faure Walker, head of the Institute for Risk and Disaster Reduction at University College London, said: "Of the deadliest earthquakes in any given year, only two in the last 10 years have been of equivalent magnitude, and four in the previous 10 years." This was a region where there had not been a major earthquake for more than 200 years or any warning signs.

On April 2, a 7.5-magnitude earthquake has hit the northeast of the Republic of China (Taiwan). According to locals, this was the strongest earthquake to hit the Island in 25 years!

On August 6 2019, the largest recorded asteroid passed close to earth "without any warning". It was the size of a football field. This asteroid passed inside the orbit of the planet Venus and back out beyond the orbit of Mars.

In December of 2023 a 7.6 earthquake struck the Philippines. There were multiple earthquakes of 7.0 + during the year of 2023. What defines an earthquake as significant are the following equations:

mag_significance = magnitude *100*(magnitude / 6.5); pager significance = red is 2000: orange is 1000: yellow is 500: green is 0; dyfi_significance = min (num_responses, 1000) * max_cdi / 10; significance = max (mag_significance, pager_significance) + dyfi_significance;

Any event with a significance > 600 is considered a significant event.

The stars of heaven falling to the ground are real meteor showers, but the stars are also angels.

This suggests that not only will physical stars fall, but angels that follow Satan "fallen angels" will come to earth in droves.

- **Israel surrounded by enemies:** An attack on Gaza by the Palestinians triggers a war with Israel. Israel's superior forces attack the Palestinians and this results in the UN and many nations and groups to cry "foul" against Israel. Israel is surrounded by nations. Iraq attacks them. Sadly, Joe Biden, the president of the US turns on Israel, while putting on a pretense of supporting them. The country is divided over support between Israel and the Palestinians. The atrocities of the Palestinians against innocent civilians in Gaza is overlooked as they protest "against Israel and the atrocities of the Israelites". As soon as Israel begins to show an upper hand, pro-Palestinian groups and politicians want a "cease fire", but they didn't want this when the Palestinians showed strength.

The actions of the US against Israel have resulted in major weather catastrophes in America. Tornados of epic proportions hit central U.S. Major Snow storms cripples the country.

In December 2023, a Turkish speaker died suddenly after claiming that Israel would suffer the "wrath of God", only he was talking about the Wrath of Allah, not HaShem: "Even if history remains silent, the truth will not remain silent. They think that if they get rid of us (Muslims), there will be no problem," he said in a translation of his speech. "However, if you get rid of us, you will not be able to escape the torment of conscience. Even if you escape the torment of history, you will not be able to escape the wrath of God (Allah)."

Immediately after making the remarks he turned and collapsed onto the floor as people rushed in to help him. There will be multitudes who will refute that this was the result of HaShem's wrath, trying to put it down to "natural causes". The immediacy of this action after blaspheming HaShem is not coincidental.

- **Winds held back:** (KJ-Revelation) "{7:1} *and after these things* I saw four angels standing on the four corners of the earth, holding the four winds of the earth, that the wind should not blow on the earth, nor on the sea, nor on any tree. {7:2} And I saw another angel ascending from the east, having the seal of the living God: and he cried with a loud voice to the four angels, to whom it was given to hurt the earth and the sea, {7:3} Saying, hurt not the earth, neither the sea, nor the trees, till we have sealed the servants of our God in their foreheads. {7:4} and I heard the number of them which were sealed: [and there were] sealed a hundred [and] forty [and] four thousand of all the tribes of the children of Israel."

"After these things" tells us that Revelation 7 is chronologically after the opening of the first 6 seals. "After this" in

Greek is "meta tauta". Referring to after the things of the Assemblies that Yochanan saw in a vision. The Revelation was given to Yochanan in more than 40 individual visions and / or sounds that he saw and heard, in a series of six units. Those six units are separated by the phrase, "After these things", which also occurs at 7: 1, 7: 9, 15: 5, and 18: 1. The first unit of Revelation to Yochanan is contained in 1: 1-3: 22; the second unit is 4: 1-7: 8; the third unit is 7: 1-7: 8; the fourth unit is 7: 9-15: 4; the fifth unit is 15: 5-17: 18; and the sixth unit is 18: 1-22: 21.

Some interpret that the words "after these things" does not refer to chronology but to a point of view. The end of 9:12 indicates a change of time periods. The interpretation of the Yovel opening of the seals does not need to refer to point of view and supports a chronological timeline for the sealing of the 144,000.

Ezekiel is told to prophesy to the *winds after a great earthquake* to give life to the dry bones. (LXXTR-Ezekiel) "37:7 so I prophesied as I was commanded: and as I prophesied, there was a noise, and, behold, an earthquake (Earthquake of seal 6); and the bones came together, bone to its bone. 37:8 And I beheld, and, lo, there were sinews upon them, and flesh came up, and skin covered them above; but there was no breath in them. 37:9 Then said he to me, Prophesy to the wind, prophesy, son of man, and say to the wind, thus says the Lord Yehovah: Come from the four winds, O breath, and breathe upon these slain, that they may live." This is referring to the opening of seal 7.

(Malachi 3:2, "But who can abide the day of his coming? And who shall stand when he appears?" "Neither their silver nor their gold shall be able to deliver them in the day of Yahweh's wrath." - Zephaniah 1:18. Zephaniah also tells how it is you can hide from Yahweh's anger, in 2:3- "Seek ye Yahweh, all ye meek of the earth that have kept his ordinances; seek righteousness, seek meekness: it may be ye will be hid in the day of Yahweh's anger." Jesus said the meek shall inherit the earth.)

(LXXNT-Revelation) "¹ After this (after the earthquake) I saw four angels standing at the four points of the earth, holding back the four winds of the earth, so that no wind would blow upon the earth, or upon the sea or upon any tree. ² And I saw another angel rising up from the east, holding the seal of the living God, and he cried out in a very great voice toward the four angels to whom *the orders* had been given to harm the earth and the sea, ³ saying, "Do not harm the earth or the sea or the trees until we have sealed the servants of our God on their foreheads."[4] And I heard the number of the ones sealed, 144,000, sealed from every tribe of the sons of Israel: [5] from the tribe of Judah twelve thousand were sealed, from the tribe of Reuben twelve thousand, from the tribe of Gad twelve thousand, [6] from the tribe of Asher twelve thousand, from the tribe of Naphtali twelve thousand, from the tribe of Manasseh twelve thousand, [7] from the tribe of Simeon twelve thousand, from the tribe of Levi twelve thousand, from the tribe of Issachar twelve thousand, [8] from the tribe of Zebulun twelve thousand, from the tribe of Joseph twelve thousand, from the tribe of Benjamin twelve thousand were sealed." Joseph is listed twice, once for Manasseh and once for Jacob. Ephraim and Dan aren't listed both of which were deported out by Assyria.

(MTJ-Revelation) "After this I saw arba'ah malachim ("angels") taking their stand on the arbah pinot ha'aretz ("the four corners of the earth"), holding the four winds of ha'aretz ("the earth") so that wind should not blow on ha'aretz ("the earth") nor on the yam ("sea") nor on any etz ("tree"). [YESHAYAH 11:12; YIRMEYAH 49:36; YECHEZKEL 37:9; DANIEL 7:2; ZECHARYAH 6:5] |2| And I saw another malach ("angel") coming up from the rising of the shemesh ("sun"), having a chotam ("seal") of the Elohim Chayyim ("Living G-ds"), and he cried with a kol Gadol ("loud voice") to the four malachim ("angels"). These were the malachim to whom it was given to harm ha'aretz ("the earth") and hayam ("the seas"), |3| Saying, Do not harm ha'aretz ("the earth") nor hayam ("the sea") nor haetzim ("the trees"), until we have marked with the chotam ("seal") the avadim ("servants") of Eloheinu upon their metsakhim ("foreheads"). [YECHEZKEL 9:4] |4| And I heard the mispar ("number") of the ones having been sealed, 144,000, having been marked with the chotam ("seal") from kol shivtei Bnei Yisroel ("every tribe of the Sons of Israel"), |5| Of the shevet of Yehudah (Judah), 12,000 having been sealed; of the shevet of Re'uven, 12,000, of the shevet of Gad, 12,000, |6| Of the shevet of Asher, 12,000, of the shevet of Naphtali, 12,000, of the shevet of M'nasheh, 12,000, |7| Of the shevet of Shim'on, 12,000, of the shevet of Levi, 12,000, of the shevet of Yissass'khar, 12,000, |8| Of the shevet of Z'vulun, 12,000, of the shevet of Yosef, 12,000, of the shevet of Binyamin, 12,000."

Joseph is listed twice. Dan and Ephraim are both missing.

John 6: 27, "Labor not for the meat which perishes, but for that meat which endures unto everlasting life, which the Son of man shall give unto you: for him hath YHWH the Father sealed". 2 Corinthians 1: 22, "Who hath also sealed us, and given the earnest of the Ruach in our hearts". Ephesians 1: 13, "In whom ye also trusted, after that ye heard the word of truth, the gospel of your salvation: in whom also after that ye believed, ye were sealed with that Ruach HaKodesh of promise"; and Ephesians 4: 30, "And grieve not the Ruach HaKodesh of YHWH, whereby ye are sealed unto the day of redemption."

This seems to indicate a figurative seal. It is not known for certain if this "mark" is literal or figurative ("only heavenly beings can see it"). This is opposed to the Mark of the Beast which is very literal and very visible. The Mark of the Beast needs to be seen before a person can do business.

The winds are held back by the angels. Wind is a residue of earth's rotation. It seems that upon the opening of this seal, the earth stops rotating. This would indicate a cosmic force acting on the earth. This goes along with seal 6 where many cosmological events are taking place. It is unknown how long the angels hold the winds, but we know it is long enough for the sealing of the elect of the tribes of Israel.

- **Those sealed by God:** (Note that Joseph is represented here twice, as his own name in verse 8 and as his son Manasseh here in verse 6. Israel only had 12 sons, so if Joseph is here twice, that means that one of the other sons of Israel is missing. Dan is missing. Of the 144000 marked, the sons of Dan will not be included.)"

(KJ-Ezekiel 7) "{7:1} Moreover the word of the LORD came unto me, saying, {7:2} Also, thou son of man, thus says the Lord GOD unto the land of Israel; An end, the end is come upon the four corners of the land (the four corners where the angels were holding back the wind). "{7:8} now will I shortly pour out my fury upon thee (the vials are poured out on the earth), and accomplish mine anger upon thee: and I will judge thee according to thy ways, and will recompense thee for all thine abominations.";"{7:11} Violence is risen up into a rod of wickedness: none of them [shall remain,] nor of their multitude, nor of any of theirs: neither [shall there be] wailing for them."

Ezekiel 38:1: The prophecy of Ezekiel against Gog and Magog. I have called you into arms and in future years you will invade a land recovered from war. They had been brought out from the nations and now live in safety. You will advance like a storm. You will devise a scheme and will attack a peaceful unsuspecting people. In that day, you will come from your place in the far north and many nations with you. I will bring you against my land. *At that time, there will be a great earthquake in Israel* (this is probably between the opening of seal 6 and 7). The mountains will be overturned and every wall will crumble. Every man's sword will be against his brother and I will pour down torrents of rain, hailstones, and burning sulfur. I will bring you (Gog and Magog) from the far north against the mountains of Israel and on the mountains of Israel, you will fall. I will give you as food to all kinds of carrion. I will send fire on Magog and those living in safety in the coastlands. Then those who live in Israel will use the weapons for fuel for 7 years, in the Valley of Hamon Gog (Hordes of Gog). For 7 months, Israel will bury the dead and men will be employed to clean the land. Every kind of bird will feed there."

Currently, Israel is in a war with practically everyone, including Gog and Magog. Even the U.S. has turned away from Israel due to the attacks with Gaza. This is the "recovering from war" of Ezekiel.

These 144,000 might not be from the actual land of Israel, but might be from among the nations where such remnants have assimilated into the world due to being taken from Israel by Assyria and later by Babylon. Israel and Judah are united as one, at this time. This marking of 12 tribes would not be possible or even necessary if they have already been raptured out of the earth. The 144,000 are sealed servants of our God on their foreheads. It does not say that they are residents of the new Nation of Israel, but that they were from the remnants of the 12 tribes. Joseph is listed twice to fulfill the 12 tribes. The other factor is that once one becomes a true Messianic Believer, they are "adopted" into the family of Abraham, so limiting these to descendants of Abraham does not exclude new "believers".

Pastor Melissa Scott made mention that Dan was a serpent according to the blessings given to him. Dan was a traveler by ships and traveled to faraway lands of land of the Celts, and into the Scandinavian countries. ("Den" mark) is probably a subsidiary of the

Tribe of Dan. They even have the same flags. Dan is not included in the sealing of the elect.

The Temple has yet to be built, so it is proposed that during this week of years (seal 6), the Temple will be restored as it was in the days of Darius of Persia. It took 5 years to rebuild the Temple in his rule, and that was without the modern technology.

According to Ezekiel and the opening of seal 6, the final regathering of Israel is waiting on the 4 winds to be released which is waiting on the 144,000 sealed of Hashem. This is to be accompanied by great earthquakes like the earth has never known. The heavens will pour down meteorites. And the revolution of the earth will be shaken from its current course in the solar system.

Rev 9: 4 "And it was commanded them that they should not hurt the grass of the earth, neither any green thing, neither any tree; but only those men which have not the seal of Elohim in their foreheads." If the earth does not rotate, the greenery mentioned would not be damaged by wind or storms as if often the case in heavy storms and wind.

Once the chosen are sealed: "and the king sealed it with his own signet, and with the signet of his lords; that the purpose *might not be changed* concerning Daniel." A seal upon anyone from God cannot be changed.

The sign of Abraham, circumcision, could not be changed. Once the family member was circumcised, he was counted as a permanent member of righteousness. The seals of the scroll were to prevent the scroll from being changed.

- **Last Babylonian Empire:** The Anti-Christ removes 3 of the ruling kings in Europe, Greece and Egypt is among of them. It is possible that Egypt is destroyed during this 7-year period of time and ceases to exist. The Club of Rome created the Ten Global Area Confederacy – the beginning of the last stage of the prophetic world Empire.

- **Multitude stands before God:** (KJ-Revelation) "{7:9} *after this* (after these events have taken place shows chronological order to the verses) I beheld, and, lo, a great multitude, which no man could number, of all nations, and kindred's, and people, and tongues, stood before the throne, and before the Lamb, clothed with white robes, and palms in their hands; {7:10} And cried with a loud voice, saying, Salvation to our God which sits upon the throne, and unto the Lamb. {7:11} And all the angels stood round about the throne, and [about] the elders and the four beasts, and fell before the throne on their faces, and worshipped God, {7:12} Saying, amen: Blessing, and glory, and wisdom, and thanksgiving, and honor, and power, and might, [be] unto our God for ever and ever. Amen. {7:13} and one of the elders answered, saying unto me, what are these which are arrayed in white robes? And whence came they? {7:14} and I said unto him, Sir, thou know. And he said to me, these are they which came out of great tribulation, and have washed their robes, and made them white in the blood of the Lamb. {7:15} therefore are they before the throne of God, and serve him day and night in his temple: and he that sits on the throne shall dwell among them. {7:16} they shall hunger no more, neither thirst anymore; neither shall the sun light on them, nor any heat. {7:17} For the Lamb which is in the midst of the throne shall feed them, and shall lead them unto living fountains of waters: and God shall wipe away all tears from their eyes."

(LXX-Revelation) "9 After these things I looked, and behold, a great multitude, which no one could count, from every nation and tribe and people and language, standing before the throne and before the Lamb, dressed in white robes, and palm branches in their hands; 10 and they are shouting out with a loud voice, saying, "Salvation is with our God who sits on the throne, and with the Lamb!" 11 and all the angels had stood in a circle around the throne and around the elders and the four living beings, and they fell on their faces before the throne and worshiped God, 12 saying, "Amen. Blessing and glory and wisdom and thanks and honor and power and strength be to our God for ever and ever. Amen." 13 And one of the elders responded saying to me, "These wearing the white robes, who are they, and where did they come from?" 14 And I spoke to him, "My lord, you know." And he said to me, "These are those coming out ("coming out-present and imperfect tense meaning this is happening or will happen in future", STRG2064) of the great tribulation ("thlipsis- pressure, afflicted, persecution", STRG2347), and they have washed their robes and made them white in the blood of the Lamb. 15 Because of this they are before the throne of God, and they serve him day and night in his temple, and the One sitting on the throne will spread his tent over them. 16 No longer will they hunger, neither will they thirst any more, nor will the sun attack them nor any scorching heat. ¹⁷ For the Lamb that is in the midst of the throne will shepherd them, and he will lead them to the springs of the waters of life; and God will wipe away every tear from their eyes." (Isaiah 49:10, 13; Isaiah 25:8)

The multitude seems to be a future look at all those who have been given a white robe of Salvation. The words in the LXX makes this point: "These are those coming out ("coming out-present and imperfect tense meaning this is happening or will happen in future", STRG2064) of the great tribulation"

(MTJ) "|9| After these things I looked, and, Hinei, a great multitude, which to number no one was being able, out of every nation and from shevatim ("tribes") and haumim ("the peoples") and lashonot ("tongues"), standing before the Kes ("Throne") and before the SEH ("Lamb", *SHEMOT 12:3; YESHAYAH 53:7 Moshiach*), each clothed with a kittel and lulavim in their hands. |10| and they cried with a kol gadol ("loud voice"), saying, Yeshu'at Eloheinu is of Hashem, our G-d, the One sitting on the Kes ("Throne"), and of the SEH ("Lamb", *SHEMOT 12:3; YESHAYAH 53:7 Moshiach*). |11| And all the malachim stood around the Kes ("Throne") and the Zekenim ("Elders", SHEMOT 12:21) and the Arbah Chayyot and they fell before the Kes ("Throne") on their faces and they worshiped Hashem, saying, [TEHILLIM 3:8] |12| Omein, the bracha ("blessing") and the kavod ("glory") and the chochmah ("wisdom") and the hodayah ("thanksgiving") and the hod ("honor") and the oz ("power") and the gevurah ("strength") be to Hashem Eloheinu l'Olelamei Olamim. Omein. |13| and one of the Zekenim ("Elders", SHEMOT 12:21) answered, saying to me, these ones, each wearing a kittel, who are they and from where did they come? |14| And I said to him, Adoni, you have da'as. And he said to me, these are the ones coming out of HaTzarah HaGedolah ("The Great Tribulation", Matthew. 24:29f) and each washed his kittel and whitened it in the dahm of the SEH ("Lamb", *SHEMOT 12:3; YESHAYAH 53:7 Moshiach*). |15| Therefore, they are before the Kes ("Throne") of Hashem and serve Him yomam valailah in His Beis Hamikdash, and the One sitting on the Kes ("Throne") will pitch the tent of His Mishkan over them. [YESHAYAH 4:5] |16| they will hunger no more nor thirst nor shall the shemesh ("sun") strike them nor any scorching heat, [YESHAYAH 49:10] |17| because the SEH, ("Lamb", *SHEMOT 12:3; YESHAYAH 53:7 Moshiach*) at the center of the Kes ("Throne"), will shepherd them and will lead them to the Makor Mayim Chayyim ["Fountain, source of Living Waters," YIRMEYAH

2:13], and Hashem will wipe away every tear from their eynayim. [YESHAYAH 25:8; 35:10; 51:11; 65:19]"

(JPS-Revelation) "...they are those," he said, "who have just passed *through the great distress*, and have washed their robes and made them white in the blood of the Lamb. 15 For this reason they stand before the very throne of God, and render Him service, day after day and night after night, in His sanctuary, and He who is sitting upon the throne will shelter them in His tent."

The Greek word for "coming out" is present and imperfect. The tribulation has not occurred as of this verse. These are those who will come out of the Great Tribulation when it occurs.

"After these things..." says that after Revelation chapters 1-6 has taken place. Six seals have been opened and the great earthquake at the beginning of chapter 6 has taken place. This is the first time that the tribulation is suggested that it has taken place; the multitude who have survived the tribulation on earth.

Professor Liebenberg claims that "After this" actually means a shift in focus, not time." But a translation of the Septuagint by Robert Palmer for Revelation 7 gives the following English: "⁹After these things I looked, and behold..." There is nothing to indicate any kind of change in "focus". It is a direct reference to chronology. Liebenberg is twisting his interpretation to fit a personal agenda and then presenting this as a Jewish specific interpretation. This is a problem that only those who believe in a 7-year opening of the seals suffer. This problem does not exist in the 50-year Yovel approach to understanding the Tribulation. "After these things" points to a chronology of after the 6 seals, and after the sealing of the 144,000.

Immediately after the multitude, seal 7 is opened "in heaven". At this time, Daniel 9 says that the Anti-Christ will make a covenant with the Holy City of Jerusalem for 1 week (7 years), but halfway through this Tribulation week, he will break the covenant. (Daniel (9:25-27).

The multitude appearing before the throne of HaShem, but the Lamb is still to open one more seal yet, meaning He is still in heaven with His Father! These multitudes stand before the throne "in heaven".

- **His Elect:** (LXXTR-Matthew) "31 and he will send his angels with a loud trumpet sound, and they will gather his elect from the four winds, from one end of sky to the other."

(MTJ-Matthew) "|31| Moshiach will send his malachim with a loud blast of the Shofar, and the malachim will gather together Moshiach's Bechirim from the four winds, from one end of Shomayim to the other."

Some try to limit the words "His elect or Moshiach's Bechirim to the Tribes of Judah and Israel, but Yeshua was speaking and He was talking about "HIS elect" or all those who "believed on Him".

- **Theories about the Second Resurrection of the Dead (i.e. Rapture):** The first resurrection is when Yeshua came from the grave after the crucifixion. He is the first born of the resurrected.

Once Yeshua opens the seventh seal, He is no longer bound to stay in heaven with the scroll. He is free to "claim his bride" often referred to as the Rapture.

(KJ- Matthew) "{24:29} immediately after the tribulation of those days shall the sun be darkened, and the moon shall not give her light, and the stars shall fall from heaven, and the powers of the heavens shall be shaken: {24:30} And then shall appear the sign of the Son of man in heaven: and then shall all the tribes of the earth mourn, and they shall see the Son of man coming in the clouds of heaven with power and great glory. {24:31} and he shall send his angels with a great sound of a trumpet, and they shall gather together his elect from the four winds, from one end of heaven to the other."

This tells us that the rapture or second resurrection of the dead will take place after seal 7 is opened and the scroll becomes the property of Yeshua.

(LXXNT –Matthew) "29 And immediately after the tribulation of those days, the sun will be darkened and the moon will not give its glow, and the stars will fall from heaven, and the forces of the heavens will be shaken. 30 And then the sign of the Son of Man will appear in the sky, and at that time, all the tribes of the land will mourn, and they will see the Son of Man coming on the clouds of the sky, with great power and great glory. 31 And he will send his angels with a loud trumpet, and they will gather his elect from the four winds, from one end of sky to the other."

After this verse in Matthew is the parable about the 10 virgins some of who were not prepared for the coming of the Lord. These verses in Matthew tell us that the Son of Man shall come in the clouds *immediately* after the tribulation of those days.

This causes a problem for the 7 years interpretation. Those in white have come "out of the tribulation", but seal 7 has not been opened yet. The JPS says ""who have just passed *through the great distress.*" This distress has been interpreted as tribulation in the translations of the LXX, the LV, and the KJ. This causes a problem with the single week of tribulation for all 7 seals as well. The tribulation is supposedly not finished at the time of the multitude standing before the throne of God.

- **Christ is risen:** When Christ rose again on day 3 after His crucifixion, He brought to life Old Testament "Messianic Believers" (from Abraham up to the Crucifixion). This is referred to as the "First Resurrection". Christ is considered the "first fruits" of the resurrection. While Lazarus was raised from the dead, and the child in the days of Elijah, both Lazarus and the child had to "die again". With the resurrection of Christ, He "cannot" die again. He is truly the first fruits of the resurrection of the dead and with Him, he "conquered death". The fist rapture of the OT saints were done in GREAT secret, and because of the rule of the Principle of First Use in Scripture, the second rapture of the NT believers therefore must ALSO happen in GREAT secret.

- **Seventh Seal:** (KJ-Revelation) "1 and when he opened the seventh seal, there was silence in heaven for about half an hour. 2 And I saw the seven angels which stand before God, and seven trumpets were given to them. 3 And another angel came and stood at the altar, holding a golden censer, and many incenses were given to him so that he might present the prayers of all the saints at the golden altar which is before the throne. 4 And the smoke of the incenses went up before God from the hand of the angel mingled with the prayers of the saints. 5 And the angel took the censer and filled it with the burning incense, and he hurled it to the earth; and there came voices and rumblings and peals of thunder and an earthquake. 6 And the seven angels who had the seven trumpets readied themselves to play."

(LXXNT-Revelation) "¹ and when he opened the seventh seal, there was silence in heaven for about half an hour. ² And I saw the seven angels which stand before God, and seven trumpets were given to them. ³ and another angel came and stood at the altar, holding a golden censer, and many incenses were given to him so that he might present the prayers of all the saints at the golden altar which is before the throne. ⁴ and the smoke of the incenses went up before God from the hand of the angel mingled with the prayers of the saints. ⁵ and the angel took the censer and filled it with the burning incense, and he hurled it to the earth; and there came rumblings and voices and peals of thunder, and an earthquake. ⁶ and the seven angels who had the seven trumpets readied themselves to play."

(MTJ-Revelation) "And when the SEH, ("Lamb", *SHEMOT 12:3; YESHAYAH 53:7 Moshiach*) opened the chotam hashevi'i ("seventh seal"), there was silence in Shomayim about half an hour. |2| And I saw the shivat hamalachim ("seven angels") who stand before Hashem, and there were given to them shivah shofarot ("trumpets"). |3| And another malach came and stood at the Mizbe'ach ("altar"), having a golden mikteret ("fire pan"), and there was given to him much ketoret ("incense", TEHILLIM 141:2) to offer with the tefillos ("prayers") of all the Kadoshim ("saints") at the golden Mizbe'ach before the Kes ("Throne"). [SHEMOT 30:1-6] |4| and the smoke of the ketoret ascended with the tefillos of the Kadoshim out of the hand of the malach ("angel") before Hashem. [TEHILLIM 141:2] |5| and the malach has taken the mikteret and filled it from the eish ("fire") of the Mizbe'ach ("altar") and he threw it down to ha'aretz, and there were thunders and sounds and lightning and an earthquake. [VAYIKRA 16:12, 13] |6| and the shivat hamalachim ("seven angels") having the shiva shofarot prepared themselves that they might sound the shofarot."

There was silence for half an hour. It is unknown if this is a figurative half an hour or a real half an hour of 30 minutes. The fire pans held the prayers of the saints for this time before the angels threw their fire pans down to earth. This starts the tribulation (according to theory 2 of the Yovel interpretation). It is unknown where this fits in according to theory 1 of 1 seven-year period. A half an hour is 30 minutes in Western time, and 540 chalakim in Hebrew time.

Chronologically Satan has not been cast out of heaven yet and the angels hold the 7 trumpets which are yet to sound out.

Seven angels stand before HaShem holding trumpets. When the angel holding the incense threw it to earth, another huge earthquake took place on earth. This earthquake is larger than the earthquake between seal 5 and 6.

The interpretation for the 1 week of years (Theory 1) of all the seals being opened shows that this "tribulation" has not ended yet, having 7 trumpets and vials with which to show the Wrath of God on earth. This seal could not have been opened in year 1 of the tribulation week, as all the other seals had to take place. There is no way to know when this seal was opened, except that it is known that Satan has not yet been cast out of heaven (3 and 1 half years into this last week). This means that this seal is still within the first half of the tribulation week, by this interpretation. One possibility is that several seals and \ or trumpets happened almost simultaneously. The last few seals and events before this have started with "And after these things..." meaning that there is still a chronological progression of the events of the seals.

The interpretation of the 50 years (Theory 2 of scroll seals) of opening the seals has this seal being opened at the beginning of the tribulation week (week 7 of the Yovel Cycle) and the trumpets and vials have to be opened. Like the other interpretation, Satan is still in heaven, but this doesn't cause a problem with this interpretation.

Date by Yovel years: 5993 - 5999 A.T. by MT;

7317 - 7423 A.T. by LXX;

(c.?) 2930 - 2936 C.E. By Julian)

- **Two Witnesses:** (KJ-Revelation) "{11:1} and there was given me a reed like unto a rod: and the angel stood, saying, Rise, and measure the temple of God, and the altar, and them that worship therein. {11:2} But the court which is without the temple leave out, and measure it not; for it is given unto the Gentiles: and the holy city shall they tread under foot forty [and] two months. {11:3} and I will give [power] unto my two witnesses, and they shall prophesy a thousand two hundred [and] threescore days, clothed in sackcloth. {11:4} these are the two olive trees, and the two candlesticks standing before the God of the earth. {11:5} and if any man will hurt them, fire proceeds out of their mouth, and devours their enemies: and if any man will hurt them, he must in this manner be killed. {11:6} these have power to shut heaven that it rains not in the days of their prophecy: and have power over waters to turn them to blood, and to smite the earth with all plagues, as often as they will. {11:7} and when they shall have finished their testimony, the beast that ascends out of the bottomless pit shall make war against them, and shall overcome them, and kill them. {11:8} and their dead bodies [shall lie] in the street of the great city, which spiritually is called Sodom and Egypt, where also our Lord was crucified. {11:9} and they of the people and kindred's and tongues and nations shall see their dead bodies three days and a half, and shall not suffer their dead bodies to be put in graves. {11:10} and they that dwell upon the earth shall rejoice over them, and make merry, and shall send gifts one to another; because these two prophets tormented them that dwelt on the earth. {11:11} and after three days and a half the Spirit of life from God entered into them, and they stood upon their feet; and great fear fell upon them which saw them. {11:12} and they heard a great voice from heaven saying unto them, Come up hither. And they ascended up to heaven in a cloud; and their enemies beheld them."

(LXXNT-Revelation) "[1] and a reed was given to me, like a measuring rod, as he (A singular masculine subject; it must be God speaking, because later in v. 3 the speaker says, "I will give authority to my two witnesses") was saying Get up, and measure the temple of God along with the altar and those worshiping in it. [2] and the outer courtyard of the temple you shall exclude, and not measure it, for it has been given to the Gentiles, and they will trample on the holy city for forty-two months. [3] And I will give *authority* to my two witnesses, and they will prophesy for 1,260 days clothed in sackcloth." [4] These are the two olive trees and the two lampstands which stand before the Lord ("theos - supreme deity", STRG2316) of the earth (Zechariah 4:3, 14 these two lampstands are Elijah and Enoch, the two human beings who never died. Their flames never went out; they are witnesses who have never slept in the grave, eyes that have never closed.). [5] and if anyone wants to harm them, fire comes from their mouth and consumes their enemies. And if anyone would want to harm them, this is how he ought to be killed. [6] These have the authority to shut up the sky so that no rain will fall during the days of their prophesying, and they have authority over the waters to turn them into blood, and to strike the earth with any kind of plague as often as they wish. ⁷ and when they complete their witness, the beast ("therion - beast, wild beast", STRG2342) coming up out of the bottomless pit will make war with them, and will conquer them and kill them. ⁸ and their corpses *lie* on the boulevard of the great city which is spiritually named Sodom and Egypt, where also their Lord was crucified. ⁹ and from peoples and tribes and languages and nations they see their corpses for three and a half days. And they are not allowing their corpses to be placed in a grave. ¹⁰ and those dwelling on the earth rejoice (The Textus Receptus has the future indicative rather than the present indicative of rejoice, and the Byzantine has the present. Yet, the Byzantine has the future indicative for the next verb, celebrate, but the present for "they see" in v. 9) over them, and celebrate, and will send gifts ("they will send") to one another. For these two prophets had tormented those dwelling on the earth. ¹¹ and after three and a half days, the breath of life from God went into them, and they stood up on their feet. And great fear fell over those watching them. ¹² and they heard a great voice from heaven saying to them, "Come up here." And they went up into heaven in a cloud, and their enemies watched them. ¹³and in that hour ("hora- hour, instant", STRG5610) a great earthquake took place, and one tenth of the city collapsed, and 7,000 people were killed. And the survivors were terrified, and they gave glory to the God of heaven."

(MTJ-Revelation) "And a measuring rod like a staff was given to me, saying, Come and measure the Beis Hamikdash of Hashem and the Mizbe'ach ("altar") and the ones worshiping there. [YECHEZKEL 40:3] |2| But do not measure the outer court of the Beis Hamikdash; leave that out, and measure it not, for it was given over to the Goyim, and the Ir HaKodesh they will trample upon arba'im and shenayim chodashim. [YECHEZKEL 40:17, 20; DANIEL 7:25; 12:7] |3| And I will give to my Sh'ney HaEdim ("TwoWitnesses") and they will speak divrei haNevu'ah ("words of prophecy") one thousand two hundred and sixty days (this is 3 and 1 half year if the year is 360 days long) having been clothed in sakkim ("sackcloth"). [BERESHIS 37:34; SHMUEL BAIS 3:31; NECHEMYAH 9:1] |4| these are the two olive trees and the two menorot standing before the Adon kol ha'aretz. [TEHILLIM 52:8; YIRMEYAH 11:16; ZECHARYAH 4:3, 11, 14] |5| and if anyone wants to harm them, eish ("fire") comes out of their mouth and destroys their oyevim ("enemies"); and if anyone wants to harm them, it is necessary for him to be killed like this. [SHMUEL BAIS 22:9; MELACHIM BAIS 1:10;

YIRMEYAH 5:14; BAMIDBAR 16:29, 35] |6| these have the samchut ("authority") to shut Shomayim that no geshem (rain) may fall during the days of their nevu'ah ("prophecy"). And samchut ("authority") they have over the waters to turn them into dahm and to strike ha'aretz with makkot ("plagues") of every kind, as often as they want. [SHEMOT 7:17, 19 [MELACHIM ALEF 17:1] |7| and when they complete the edut ("testimony") of them, the Chayyah ("Beast, Anti- Moshiach") coming up from the Tehom ("Abyss") will make war with them and will conquer them and will kill them. [DANIEL 7:21] |8| And the NEVELAH ("corpse", DEVARIM 21:23) of them will be on the rekhov ("street") of the Ir Hagadol, which, spiritually, is called S'dom and Mitzrayim ("Egypt"), where also the Adon of them was pierced on the etz. [YESHAYAH 1:9; YIRMEYAH 13:14; YECHEZKEL 16:46] |9| And some of haummmim ("the peoples") and shevatim ("tribes") and leshonot ("languages") and Goyim ("Nations") see the NEVELAH of them for shloshah and a half yamim and the NEVELAH of them they do not permit to be put into a kever ("tomb"). [TEHILLIM 79:2, 3] |10| and the ones dwelling on ha'aretz ("the earth") rejoice with great simcha ("joy") over them and make merry and they will send matanot (gifts) to one another, because these two nevi'im ("prophets") tormented the ones dwelling on ha'aretz ("the earth"). [Nehemiah 8:10, 12; Esther 9:19, 22] |11| and after the shloshah ("three") and a half yamim ("days"), a Ruach of Chayyim from Hashem entered into them, and they stood up upon their feet, and pachad Gadol ("great terror") fell upon the ones seeing them. [YECHEZKEL 37:5, 9, 10, 14] |12| and they heard a kol gadol ("loud voice") out of Shomayim saying to them, "Come up here!" And they went up into Shomayim in the anan ("cloud"), and their oyevim ("enemies") saw them. [MELACHIM BAIS 2:11] |13| and in that hour occurred a great earthquake and the tenth part of the city fell and there were killed in the earthquake shivat alafim ("seven thousand"), and the rest became afraid and gave kavod ("glory") to Elohei HaShomayim."

The two witnesses are dressed in sackcloth, which is a garb worn in a time of mourning. They are in mourning for the people of the tribulation.

This verse does not start with "And after these things". This is the first time where chronology is reversed back to the beginning of Seal 7, or the beginning of the Tribulation. This event takes up the first 3 and a half years of the tribulation. They start in year 1 so this event must go back in time before the first seal according to Theory 1 (7 years of Revelation) (by 1 week of year's interpretation).

By the Yovel interpretation (50-year interpretation-Yovel interpretation), this does not present a problem, as they appear at the beginning of seal 7.

Many will believe these 2 to be evil because of the destruction they bring. The witnesses will resume preaching the *Gospel of the Kingdom* which was started by John the Baptist. For the next 7 years, the Anti-Christ will blaspheme the Holy One. These 2 witnesses are the 2 olive trees and the 2 lampstands that stand before HaShem. They will call a famine for the entire term of their witness and they have power to turn water to blood (the first plague from the time of the Exodus) and to strike the earth with every plague. They have free will as they can turn the water to blood "as they will".

There are two people who have never seen the first "death"; Enoch ben Yared and Elijah the Prophet in the time of Ahab. It is likely that the two witnesses are these two and as a result, they will experience the "first death" as all men are supposed to do, except those who are alive at the end of days. One other possibility is Moses as no one knows where his grave is. The verses in Deuteronomy make it plain that Moses passed his mantel on to Joshua and then died at age 120 (Deuteronomy 34). His body was hidden by the angels, but he experienced the first death. Yeshua hinted that Elijah would be coming "again", after the Transfiguration (Mark 9) These plagues are in addition to the plagues of the seals. The opening of the 6 seals takes place before the 2 witnesses, giving more support for a 50-year period of the seals, where the first 6 seals are opened in years 1 – 42 of the Yovel cycle and are not part of the Tribulation Week. For those who interpret the seals all being opened in 1 week of 7 years, the 2 witnesses are alive during the opening of all 7 seals. The trumpets are opened in the first half of the Tribulation as well as they come before Satan is cast out and before the 2 witnesses are taken to heaven.

"And when they complete their witness, the beast ("therion – beast, wild beast", STRG2342) coming up out of the bottomless pit will make war with them, and will conquer them and kill them." This says that at the *end* of their testimony the beast will come out of the bottomless pit (at the middle of the week of tribulation). This is often interpreted to be the Anti-Christ, but the Anti-Christ is believed to attain his kingdom at the beginning of the tribulation and at the beginning of the testimony of the two witnesses, possibly even sooner, as he must rule over the 10 kingdoms or 10 toes of the image of Nebuchadnezzar. This "beast" is the anti-Christ only in the Yovel interpretation of the tribulation.

Daniel says that the Anti-Christ will make a covenant with Israel for 1 week of years. With the 1-week interpretation, this covenant takes place before the opening of the seals. With the Yovel interpretation, this covenant starts with the opening of seal 7 and does not present any problem. Halfway through the tribulation, the covenant is broken. This will take place when Satan is cast out of heaven and commits the abomination of desolation in the Temple.

Their bodies will lie in the streets for 3 days and the entire world will see them. Due to the invention of the internet, which is vastly spreading to the point that everyone has it, the view of their bodies will be easily possible all over the world. In the 60's and 70's, eschatologists just believed this was due to television. The witnesses will be resurrected by Ruach Elohim and taken up. This means that they have now experienced the first death as every other person who has ever lived has experienced.

It is not known for certain if "in that hour" or "in that instant" is literal or figurative, but it is likely that in this case the words are literally meant to be in that hour of time. The earthquake is the third earthquake of this huge nature (the first being between seal 5 and 6 and the second being at the beginning of seal 7). The mark of HaShem over His believers protects believers from most of the events of the seals, but they will not be protected from the earthquake here that kills 7000 people.

Both Judas and the Anti-Christ are called the Devil (John 6:70-71). He wasn't *just demon possessed.* He was the Devil incarnate. The Beast shall come from the same Abyss where Judas was sent after his death.

They are witnesses for 1260 days which is exactly 3 and 1/2 years but only if the year is 360 days long. Since in seal 6 the events were of a cosmological nature, it is likely that during seal 6, the earth will resume a 360-day year.

Dates for Witnesses: 5993.01 – 5995.06 A.T. by MT;

7417.01 – 7419.06 A.T. by LXX;

2930 – 2932 C.E. By Julian:

- **Wrath of HaShem:** The opening of seal 7 brings in the "Wrath of God". The most devastating storm in history. The four winds will now be released. A huge earthquake takes place. The silence in heaven was due to the shock of the heavenly witnesses. This is the silence before the storm.
- **Angels with Trumpets:** (KJ-Revelation) "{8:2} and I saw the seven angels which stood before God; and to them were given seven trumpets. {8:3} and another angel came and stood at the altar, having a golden censer; and there was given unto him much incense, that he should offer [it] with the prayers of all saints upon the golden altar which was before the throne. {8:4} and the smoke of the incense, [which came] with the prayers of the saints, ascended up before God out of the angel's hand. {8:5} and the angel took the censer, and filled it with fire of the altar, and cast [it] into the earth: and there were voices, and thunderings, and lightening, and an earthquake. {8:6} and the seven angels which had the seven trumpets prepared themselves to sound."

(LXXNT-Revelation) "¹and when he opened the seventh seal, there was silence in heaven for about half an hour. ²And I saw the seven angels which stand before God, and seven trumpets were given to them. ³and another angel came and stood at the altar, holding a golden censer, and many incenses were given to him so that he might present the prayers of all the saints at the golden altar which is before the throne. ⁴and the smoke of the incenses went up before God from the hand of the angel mingled with the prayers of the saints. ⁵and the angel took the censer and filled it with the burning incense, and he hurled it to the earth; and there came rumblings and voices and peals of thunder, and an earthquake. ⁶and the seven angels who had the seven trumpets readied themselves to play."

The 7 trumpets and the vials all take place during the early part of this last week regardless of which interpretation is believed.

Trumpets are warning signals, used to warn of a coming war or invasions or as a summons for the people. The angel with the golden censer brought the prayers before HaShem. On earth, the censers were offered on the incense altar just before the Holy of Holies. This same is happening here, in heaven. This censer was "thrown to earth". This was the cause of the earthquake before the Angels with the Trumpets. Judgment is coming directly from the Throne of Elohim!

It is trumpet four that is set apart with the angel calling out "Woe, Woe, Woe". Angel 5 includes the statement: "12 the first woe is past; two other woes have still to come." This definitely has the signature of a chronological order of the last 3 angels. This is not made clear in the first 4 angels of the trumpets.

**First Trumpet:** (KJ-Revelation) "{8:7} the first angel sounded, and there followed hail and fire mingled with blood, and they were cast upon the earth: and the third part of trees was burnt up, and all green grass was burnt up."

Unlike the seals, it is unlikely that these woes have human causes. That is not to say that they might have natural causes, but natural does not eliminate supernatural causes as well. The grass and trees were not allowed to be harmed earlier, but now, the trumpets bring damage to the earth. Fires will rage around the world burning up vegetation unlike anything seen before. The fire will not be a case of arson by some human, but will be from a supernatural source. There is nothing to indicate this is a result of some meteorite.

(LXXNT-Revelation) "7 and the first one sounded his trumpet; and there came hail and fire mixed with blood, and it was rained on the earth. And one third of the earth was (will be) burned up and one third of the trees were burned up, and all the green grass was burned up."

(MTJ-Revelation) "|7| and harishon sounded his shofar; and there came barad ("hail") and eish ("fire") having been mingled with dahm and it was thrown to ha'aretz, and a third of ha'aretz was burned up, and a third of the etzim ("trees") was burned up and all green grass was burned up." [YECHEZKEL 38:22 ((KJ Ezekiel) "{38:22} and I will plead against him with pestilence and with blood; and I will rain upon him, and upon his bands, and upon the many people that [are] with him, an overflowing rain, and great hailstones, fire, and brimstone.")]."

Hail and fire mixed with blood (such as was seen in the hail of fire in the plagues of Egypt at the time of Moses). This is likely from the tail of a comet which contains such fire. There is a note that there will be signs in heaven, which could allude to another large planet size comet passing by like the Planet Typhon\Venus in the days of the Exodus. If the comet is the cause of this hail fire, it will come much closer to earth than the comet at the time of the Exodus. This does not contradict the supernatural control of HaShem. This fire will be much more extensive than the hail of fire in Egypt. It will burn one third of the vegetation on earth (the side of earth that is closest to the comet).

The words "the first angel" implies that this angel blew the trumpet before the others. There really is no real proof that this is correct. Going back to Genesis 1:1-3, while HaShem broke the steps out in His transparency to explain what He did and How, yet, the verses are believed by this writer that they took place simultaneously. This could be true with the trumpets. The events triggered by each trumpet could possibly take place at the same time (but still in a semblance of order) or within a very short time. This cannot be proven either false or true by the wording of the verses.

John saw the results of the trumpets, but he does not make it clear as to any time separation of the trumpets from one another. If this is true, we have a direct correlation between the first day of creation and the trumpet(s) of destruction. The beginning is being undone by the end.

**Second Trumpet:** (KJ-Revelation) "{8:8} and the second angel sounded, and as it were a great mountain burning with fire was cast into the sea: and the third part of the sea became blood; {8:9} and the third part of the creatures which were in the sea, and had life, died; and the third part of the ships were destroyed."

(LXXNT-Revelation) "⁸and the second angel sounded his trumpet; and something like a huge mountain burning with fire was hurled into the sea. And one third of the sea was turned to blood, ⁹ and one third of the creatures that live (literally, "a third of the creatures in the sea died, those possessing souls.") in the sea died, and one third of the ships were destroyed." The ships of today are massive (aircraft carriers, battleships, and destroyers, plus all the "cruise ships".

(MTJ-Revelation) "|8| And the malach hasheyni ("second angel") sounded his shofar; and as it were a great mountain with eish ("fire") burning was thrown into the yam ("sea"), and a third of the yam became dahm |9| and a third of the living yetzurim hayam ("creatures of the sea") died, and a third of the ships were destroyed."

This mountain sounds like a meteorite that is burning up as it passes through the atmosphere but there is nothing to tell where the mountain came from. It lands in the ocean and causes major devastation to all creatures of that sea and the ships.

There is a progression appearing that matches the creation week. First the plants are created followed by the sea creatures. The first and second trumpet seem to "undo" what was created in order.

- **Third Trumpet:** (KJ-Revelation) "{8:10} and the third angel sounded, and there fell a great star from heaven, burning as it were a lamp, and it fell upon the third part of the rivers, and upon the fountains of waters; {8:11} And the name of the star is called Wormwood: and the third part of the waters became wormwood; and many men died of the waters, because they were made bitter."

(LXXNT-Revelation) "¹⁰ and the third angel sounded his trumpet; and a huge star ("astor - great star", STRG792)) fell from heaven, burning like a lamp, and it fell on a third of the rivers, and on the sources of the waters. ¹¹ and the name of the star means "Wormwood." ("Absinthos - bitterness", STRG894) And a third of the waters were turned into bitterness, and many of the people died from the waters because they were made bitter."

(MTJ-Revelation) "|10| and the malach hashlishi ("third angel") sounded his shofar; and there fell out of Shomayim a kokhav gadol ("great star") blazing as a torch and it fell on a third of the rivers and on the wells of mayim ("waters –plural"). [YESHAYAH 14:12] |11| and the name of the kokhav ("star") is said to be "Wormwood," and a third of the mayim became bitter wormwood, and many of the Bnei Adam died from the mayim because the mayim were made bitter. [YIRMEYAH 9:15, 23:15 – "therefore thus saith the Lord God of Israel, Behold, I will feed them with trouble and will cause them to drink water of gall:"]" This was the same kind of gall that was fed to Christ when He hung on the cross.

There is a continuation of progression appearing that matches the creation week. First the plants are created followed by the sea creatures. The first and second trumpet seem to "undo" what was created in order. This wormwood would poison land animals as well as humans.

Wormwood is a plant and is not poisonous by itself. This wormwood comes from a falling star (asteroid, comet, or other such rock from space.). It comes from a burning star which is indicative of an asteroid as it burns up when it enters into the atmosphere. Many men die from the bitter "fresh" infected waters on earth.

(Star Newspaper May 1996) "During President Yeltsin's recent visit to China, a comment was made by his Chinese hosts which escaped the media's attention. Pres. Yeltsin urged the Chinese to sign the comprehensive nuclear test ban treaty. Beijing refused, claiming they needed to continue to work on a bomb that could be used against an asteroid heading towards earth. The Chinese were referring to the rogue star named Wormwood. According to scientists, Wormwood is about five times larger than the earth and will pass within 40 million km, a mere stone's throw in galactic terms. The star will appear as large as a full moon; its gravitational pull will cause incredible storms, earthquakes and volcanic eruptions. Depending on the actual heat emanating from the star, the polar ice caps, oceans and rivers will turn into steam. Ultimately the earth will be ripped out of its orbit and hurled either into the sun or into the vastness of outer space. International scientists have been tracking Wormwood for the past four years. The star was located in the Oort cloud at the edge of our solar system. Calculations indicate that the star is destined to enter the solar system around the turn of this century. United States and Russian military scientists are working feverishly to build and deploy an array of nuclear missiles in the hope of blasting Wormwood from colliding with earth."

- **Fourth Trumpet:** (KJ-Revelation) "{8:12} and the fourth angel sounded, and the third part of the sun was smitten, and the third part of the moon, and the third part of the stars; so, as the third part of them was darkened, and the day shone not for a third part of it, and the night likewise. {8:13} And I beheld, and heard an *angel* flying through the midst of heaven, saying with a loud voice, Woe, woe, woe, to the inhabitants of the earth by reason of the other voices of the trumpet of the three angels, which are yet to sound!"

(JPS-Revelation) "12 Then the fourth angel blew his trumpet; and a curse fell upon a third part of the sun, a third part of the moon, and a third part of the stars, so that a third part of them were darkened and for a third of the day, and also of the night, there was no light. 13 Then I looked, and I heard a solitary eagle crying in a loud voice, as it flew across the sky, "Alas, alas, alas, for the inhabitants of the earth, because of the significance of the remaining trumpets which the three angels are about to blow!"

(LXXNT-Revelation) "¹² and the fourth angel sounded his trumpet; and a third of the sun was struck, and a third of the moon and a third of the stars, such that one third of their *light* was darkened (the verb 'was darkened' is singular) and a third of the daylight would not be shined, and the same with the night. ¹³ And I looked, and I heard an eagle ("aggelos-messenger, angel", STRG32) flying at zenith saying with a very loud voice, "Woe, woe, woe to those dwelling on the earth, because of the remaining sounds of the trumpet from the three angels about to sound!"

(MTJ-Revelation) "|12| and the malach harevi'I ("fourth angel") sounded his shofar; and a third of the Shemesh ("sun") was struck and a third of the levanah ("moon") and a third of the kokhavim ("stars"), that a third of them might be darkened, and the yom ("day") could not appear, and likewise the lailah ("night"). [SHEMOT 10:21-23; YECHEZKEL 32:7] |13| And I saw, and I heard one nesher ("eagle") flying in midair, saying with a kol Gadol ("loud voice"), Oy, oy, oy to the ones dwelling on ha'aretz ("the earth"), because of the remaining blasts of the shofar of the shloshet hamalachim (three angels) being about to sound."

There is nothing to suggest that there was any chronological time designated between the 4 trumpets, meaning that they could be all at the same time, consecutive with a short time between, or consecutive with some length of time between them. Most interpreters tend to believe that these trumpets were hours, days, or even weeks between them. This is not necessarily so. In Trumpet number 5, this changes as the locusts are given 5 months (repeated two times) to torment humans, but not kill them.

This does not follow the progression of the Creation as the sun and stars were created before the sea creatures. But this does still seem to point back to HaShem "undoing" Creation. This goes back also to when HaShem said He "repented that He had made man".

The Greek uses the word aggelos which does not translate to "eagle", yet the LXX, MTJ, LV and JSP all translate this word to eagle. The KJ translates this word to "angel". From the context, it is most likely an angel flying through the air to make this announcement.

One third of the light either suggests something huge blocking the light. One alternative is that the earth's rotation has been affected by the previous 2 trumpets (asteroids or meteorites) and the rotation is made faster so that the days and nights are 1 third shorter, being about 8 hours each for a total of a 16 hour "day". If this is true, the faster rotation will cause a large increase in storms around the globe. Global warming will no longer be an issue. The stability of the earth will be a huge question among those who do not understand the supernatural influence of the Living God.

It is relevant that the angel said "woe" three times as that is how many woes will appear in the next trumpet calls.

- **Fifth Trumpet First Woe:** (KJ-Revelation) "{9:1} and the fifth angel sounded, and I saw a star fall from heaven unto the earth: and to him was given the key of the bottomless pit. {9:2} and he opened the bottomless pit; and there arose a smoke out of the pit, as the smoke of a great furnace; and the sun and the air were darkened by reason of the smoke of the pit. {9:3} and there came out of the smoke locusts upon the earth: and unto them was given power, as the scorpions of the earth have power. {9:4} and it was commanded them that they should not hurt the grass of the earth, neither any green thing, neither any tree; but only those men which have not the seal of God in their foreheads. {9:5} and to them it was given that they should not kill them, but that they should be tormented five months: and their torment [was] as the torment of a scorpion, when he strikes a man. {9:6} and in those days shall men seek death, and shall not find it; and shall desire to die, and death shall flee from them. {9:7} and the shapes of the locusts [were] like unto horses prepared unto battle; and on their heads [were] as it were crowns like gold, and their faces [were] as the faces of men. {9:8} and they had hair as the hair of women, and their teeth were as [the teeth] of lions. {9:9} and they had breastplates, as it were breastplates of iron; and the sound of their wings [was] as the sound of chariots of many horses running to battle. {9:10} and they had tails like unto scorpions, and there were stings in their tails: and their power [was] to hurt men five months. {9:11} and they had a king over them, [which is] the angel of the bottomless pit, whose name in the Hebrew tongue [is] Abaddon, but in the Greek tongue hath [his] name Apollyon. {9:12} one woe is past; [and,] behold, there come two woes more hereafter."

The locusts do not follow the natural order of locusts that feed on greenery of the earth. These locusts do not attack the grass or trees. They are supernatural in nature, demonic in some ways, but not from fallen angels.

(JPS-Revelation) "1 The fifth angel blew his trumpet; and I saw a Star which had fallen from Heaven to the earth; and to him was given the key of the depths of the bottomless pit, 2 and he opened the depths of the bottomless pit. And smoke came up out of the pit resembling the smoke of a vast furnace, so that the sun was darkened, and the air also, by reason of the smoke of the pit. 3 And from the midst of the smoke there came locusts on to the earth, and power was given to them resembling the power which earthly scorpions possess. 4 And they were forbidden to injure the herbage of the earth, or any green thing, or any tree. They were only to injure human beings—*those who have not the seal of God on their foreheads.* 5 Their mission was not to kill, but to cause awful agony for five months; and this agony was like that which a scorpion inflicts when it stings a man. 6 And at that time people will seek death, but will not possibility find it, and will long to die, but death evades them. 7 The appearance of the locusts was like that of horses equipped for war. On their heads they had wreaths which looked like gold. 8 Their faces seemed human and they had hair like women's hair, but their teeth resembled those of lions. 9 They had breast-plates which seemed to be made of steel; and the noise caused by their wings was like that of a vast number of horses and chariots hurrying into battle. 10 They had tails like those of scorpions, and also stings; and in their tails lay their power of injuring mankind for five months. 11 The locusts had a king over them—the angel of the bottomless pit, whose name in Hebrew is 'Abaddon,' while in the Greek he is called 'Apollyon.' 12 The first woe is past; two other woes have still to come."

(LXXNT-Revelation) "1 and the fifth angel sounded his trumpet; and I saw a fallen star ("aster – star", STRG792), (That is, a fallen angel. Angels are called stars in Judges 5:20; Job 38:7; Isaiah

14:13; Daniel 8:10 / Revelation 12:4; Revelation 1:20. In this verse in Revelation, it is a "fallen star," which is another way to refer to a demon) *fallen* out of heaven onto earth, and the key to the bottomless pit had been given to him) 2 and he opened the bottomless pit ("abussos-abyss, depthless", STRG12), and smoke ascended from the pit like smoke from a burning furnace. And the sun and the sky were darkened from the smoke of the pit. 3 And from the smoke, locusts ("akris-locusts", STRG200) went out over the earth, and they were given a power like the power that the scorpions of Earth have. 4 And it was commanded them that they not harm the grass of the earth or anything green or any tree, but only humans *who do not have the seal of God on their foreheads.* 5 And orders were given them that they not kill them, but that they be tormented for five months. And their torment will be like the pain of a scorpion when it strikes a person. 6 And during those days the people will seek death, and will not find it. Yes, they will long earnestly to die, and death will elude them. 7 And the appearance of the locusts was like horses outfitted for war, and on their head's golden crowns, and their faces like human faces, 8 and they had hair like the hair of women, and their teeth were like lions' teeth, 9 and they had thoraxes like breastplates of iron, and the sound of their wings was like the sound of many chariot horses rushing to battle. 10 And they have tails like scorpions, and stingers, and in their tails, they have power to do harm to humans for five months, 11 having as king over them the angel of the Abyss. His name in Hebrew is Abbadōn ("a destroying angel", STRG3), and in Greek he has the name Apollyōn. 12 The first woe has passed. Behold, even after all this, a second woe is still coming."

(MTJ-Revelation) "And the malach hachamishi ("fifth angel") sounded his shofar; and I saw a kokhav ("star") having fallen out of Shomayim to ha'aretz. And was given to it the mafte'ach of the shaft of the Tehom ("Abyss"). |2| and he opened the shaft of the Tehom ("Abyss"), and smoke came up out of the shaft as smoke of a great furnace, and the shemesh ("Sun") was darkened and the air was darkened by the smoke of the shaft. [BERESHIS 19:28; SHEMOT 19:18; YOEL 2:2, 10] |3| and out of the smoke came forth arbeh ("locusts") to ha'aretz ("the earth"), and Samchut ("authority") was given to them like the samchut of the akrabei ha'aretz ("scorpions of the earth"). [SHEMOT 10:12-15] |4| And it was told them that they should not harm the grass of ha'aretz ("the earth") nor any greenery nor any etz ("tree"), except the Bnei Adam, all who do not have the chotam ("seal") of Hashem on their metsakhim ("foreheads") (YECHEZKEL 9:4). |5| and it was given to them that they should not kill them, but that they will be tormented chamishah chodashim ("five months"). Their torment is as the torment of an akrav when it stings a man. |6| and in those days Bnei Adam will seek Mavet ("Death") and by no means will find it. And they will desire to die and Mavet flees from them. [IYOV 3:21; 7:15; YIRMEYAH 8:3] |7| and the appearances of the arbeh ("locusts") were like susim (horses) having been prepared for milchamah ("war"), and on the heads of them what looked like atarot ("Diadems") of zahav ("gold") and the faces were like the faces of Bnei Adam. [YOEL 2:4; DANIEL 7:8] |8| And they had hair that looked like the hair of an isha ("a woman"), and they had teeth that looked like the teeth of an aryeh ("lion"), [YOEL 1:6] |9| and they had breastplates like iron breastplates and the sound of the wings of them was as the sound of many merkavot ("chariots") with susim ("horses") racing into the sadeh krav ("battlefield"), [YOEL 2:5] |10| And they have tails like akrabim ("scorpions"), with stingers, and the ko'ach ("power") of them is in their tails to harm Bnei Adam chamishah chodashim ("five months"). |11| they have over them a melech ("king"), the malach ("angel") of the Tehom ("Abyss"), the name for him in Ivrit, "Abaddon," (that is, Destruction) and in Elliniki he has the name Apollyon (that is, "Destroyer"). [IYOV 26:6; 28:22; 31:12; TEHILLIM 88:11] |12| The Oy Echad ("the First Woe") has passed. Hinei, yet comes two more woes after these things."

A time of 5 months, repeated twice, is mentioned in this woe. This angel "fell from heaven" which is suggestive that it was an emissary of Lucifer. It released tormentors to roam the earth for 5 months. The locusts are demons released to do their harm but not from fallen angels.

This refers to all mankind except those who have been sealed (144,000). This implies that even believers will be tormented who have not been sealed. This is a strong implication that the resurrection of the saints has taken place, but did not include the sealed of God. This seems to be a mystery as it is a contradiction of the understanding of the rapture or resurrection

In the 17th degree of Freemasonry, the mason must say the secret word "ABADDON" whilst being initiated from "*Moral and Dogma of Ancient and Accepted Scottish Rite Free Masonry*" by Albert Pike. There are only four angels named in the Scriptures: Michael and Gabriel (the two righteous angels from YHWH) as well as Lucifer (Satan) and Abaddon.

"|4| And it was told them that they should not harm the grass of ha'aretz ("the earth") nor any greenery nor any etz ("tree"), except the Bnei Adam, *all who do not have the chotam* ("seal") of Hashem on their metsakhim ("foreheads") (YECHEZKEL 9:4)."

If the rapture had taken place by now, this statement would not be necessary: This statement indicates that there are men on earth who have the seal of God on their foreheads! This is not dependent on which interpretation of the opening of the seals is correct. In both interpretations, this takes place toward the end of the 7 seals being opened, but still before the fall of Satan from heaven. These are supernatural locusts, like scorpions, assigned to torment anyone without the seal of HaShem. The locusts were not to kill the non-believers, but just to torment with their painful stings. The pain is so intense, that many would seek death, but not find it. This affected "all" men \ women who did not have the seal of God.

The locusts will have the likeness of warriors riding on horses, wearing crowns on their head with faces of men, hair like that of a woman, teeth like that of a lion, breastplates of iron (reminiscent of the last empire of iron before the coming of Yeshua), wings that sound like a multitude of chariots, tails like scorpions, and the authority to torment men for 5 months (150 days). They had a king who was called Abaddon (or Apollyon). He is a destroying angel. This is a literal 5 months, (150 days-the number of days the earth was under water during the Flood of Noah) not figurative. The first woe is past and 2 other woes "have yet to come". This still talks about a chronology of the events in Revelation in order of their appearance.

This angel was one of the fallen angels that followed Satan. He was not "cast out of heaven" but was a follower of Satan. At this moment in time, the followers of Satan and Lucifer as well, still have access to travel between heaven and earth. It was his assignment to let loose the scorpions on earth by HaSatan as HaSatan knew what was coming.

- **Sixth Trumpet; Second Woe:** (KJ-Revelation) "{9:13} and the sixth angel sounded, and I heard a voice from the four horns of the golden altar which is before God, {9:14} Saying to the sixth angel which had the trumpet, Loose the four angels which are bound in the great river Euphrates. {9:15} and the four angels were loosed, which were prepared for an hour, and a day, and a month, and a year, for to slay the third part of men. {9:16} and the number of the army of the horsemen [were] two hundred thousand thousand: and I heard the number of them. {9:17} and thus I saw the horses in the vision, and them that sat on them, having breastplates of fire (these were not made of iron and therefore had no relation to the Roman army), and of jacinth, and brimstone: and the heads of the horses [were] as the heads of lions; and out of their mouths issued fire and smoke and brimstone. {9:18} by these three was the third part of men killed, by the fire, and by the smoke, and by the brimstone, which issued out of their mouths. {9:19} for their power is in their mouth, and in their tails: for their tails [were] like unto serpents, and had heads, and with them they do hurt. {9:20} And the rest of the men which were not killed by these plagues yet repented not of the works of their hands, that they should not worship devils, and idols of gold, and silver, and brass, and stone, and of wood: which neither can see, nor hear, nor walk: {9:21} Neither repented they of their murders, nor of their sorceries, nor of their fornication, nor of their thefts."

The one voice coming from the altar might be the Slain Lamb of God who was from the altar of sacrifices (burnt offering). The angels that are bound must be fallen angels that serve Lucifer. Angels of HaShem are never bound. The Euphrates River was the beginning of the Cult of Nimrod in Genesis, the first rebellious empire of the world. The horsemen are demons or fallen angels, not good angels and they will kill one third of humanity. The description is not angelic in nature.

Like Pharaoh of Egypt during the last of the plagues, they were not able to repent at this point. Their free will had been removed.

(LXXNT-Revelation) "[13] and the sixth angel sounded his trumpet. And I heard a voice from the horns (4 horns -Amos 3:14 says "horns of the altar" without the number four. Moreover, the altar of incense was also golden, Exodus 39:38) of the golden altar before God, [14] saying to the sixth angel, the one holding the trumpet, "Release the four angels that are bound at the great river Euphrates." [15]and he released the four angels, held ready for that hour and day and month and year in order to kill one third of humanity. [16]and the number of their mounted troops was 200,000,000. I heard the number of them.[17] and this is how I saw the horses in the vision, and those sitting on them: Having breastplates like fire, that is, dusky red and Sulphur colored; and the heads of the horses like heads of lions, and from their mouths comes fire and smoke and Sulphur. [18] by these three plagues, of the fire and smoke and Sulphur coming from their mouths, one third of humanity was killed. [19] Now the power of the horses is in their mouths and in their tails; for their tails are like snakes, having heads, and with these they do injury. [20] And the rest of humanity, those who were not killed by these plagues, they did not repent, neither of the works of their hands, such that they worship demons and idols made of gold and silver and bronze and stone and wood, which can neither see nor hear nor walk, [21] and neither did they repent of their murders, nor their sorceries, (potions of sorcery, or witchcraft - This Greek word - phármakon or pharmakea, STRG5331 is used nowhere else in the New Testament. It's meaning in other literature ranges from poison, to magic potions and charms to medicines and drugs. The other Greek words in the N.T. derived from the same root usually pertain to sorcery and magic) nor their sexual immorality, nor their thefts."

(MTJ-Revelation) "|13| and the malach hashish ("the sixth angel") sounded his shofar. And I heard kol echad ("one voice") from the four horns of the golden Mizbe'ach ("altar") before Hashem, [SHEMOT 30:1-3] |14| saying to the malach hashishi, the one having the shofar, Release the arba'at hamalachim ("the four angels") having been bound at the great river, Euphrates. [BERESHIS 15:18; DEVARIM 1:7; YEHOSHUA 1:4; YESHAYAH 11:15] |15| and the arba'at hamalachim (four angels) were released, having been prepared for the sha'ah ("hour") and the yom ("day") and chodesh ("month") and shanah ("year"), that they should kill a third of Bnei Adam. |16| and the mispar ("number") of tziveot haparashim ("troops of cavalrymen") were twice ten thousand times ten thousand. I heard the mispar of them. |17| And thus I saw the susim ("horses") in my chazon ("vision, revelation, prophecy") and the riders on them, having breastplates fiery red and hyacinth blue and sulfur yellow, and the heads of the susim like heads of arayot ("lions"), and from the mouths of them goes forth eish ("fire") and smoke and gofrit ("sulfur"). [TEHILLIM 11:6; YESHAYAH 30:33; YECHEZKEL 38:22] |18| From these shlosh hamakkot ("three plagues"; *T.N. this word makkah, makkot [plural] comes from the Pesach Haggadah `eser makkot' or ten plagues, and is a key word from here on in the book of Revelation, showing the end time plagues of the Brit Chadasha Exodus of the Geulah Redemption*) were killed a third of Bnei Adam, by the eish ("fire") and the smoke and the gofrit ("sulfur") coming out of the mouth of them. |19| for the ko'ach ("power") of the susim ("horses") is in their mouths and in their tails, for their tails are like nechashim ("serpents"), having heads, and with them they inflict harm. |20| And the rest of the Bnei Adam, the ones not killed by these makkot ("plagues"), did not make teshuva ("repentance") and turn from the ma'asim ("deeds") of their hands or forsake worship of shedim ("demons") and the itztzavim ("idols, images, tzelamim"), those of gold and of silver and of bronze and of stone and of wood, which neither are able to see nor to hear nor to walk. [DEVARIM 4:28; 31:29; YIRMEYAH 1:16; MICHOH 5:13] |21| and they did not make teshuva ("repentance, turning from sin to G-d") of the retzichot ("murders") of them nor of the kishufim ("sorceries") of them nor of the zenunim ("fornication") of them nor of the gneyvot ("thefts") of them. [YESHAYAH 47:9, 12]"

The word for sorceries is related to "pharmakeia", which refers to potions and drugs. The increase use of drugs has taken over around the world. South American cartels and Oriental Triads had increased their sale of the drugs. It would appear to us that the US is their main target, but this isn't so. In Europe and other continents, drug use has escalated tremendously. Drug addicts fill the streets of cities around the world.

The words are 'held ready for that hour and day and month and year". When Yeshua says that no man knows the "day and hour" of His return He did not include the month and year as it is included here. This verse confirms that the interpretation of Yeshua's words are *exactly* what He intended to say and mean (no more and no less). Assuming that Yeshua intended to add the words, month and year is a wrong assumption.

In spite of the horror mankind was going through, they refused to repent of the work of their hands. The appeal to repent has ceased and there is no cry to repent. As in the case of the Pharaoh in the time of Moses, the free choice to repent has been removed. While the images given here would be enough to scare men, it is likely that the common man was not able to see or hear the riders or the locusts of the first woe as spiritual men being blind to the Word of God as they were. They would likely put this down to some plague that they cannot cure and very likely that they would blame HaShem for their torment and for the many deaths.

According to Ezekiel the final regathering of Israel is waiting on the 4 winds to be released which is waiting on the 144000 sealed of HaShem. This is to be accompanied by great earthquakes like the earth has never known. The heavens will pour down meteorites. And the revolution of the earth will be shaken from its current course in the solar system.

- **Another mighty angel (Little Scroll):** (KJ-Revelation) "{10:1} And I saw another mighty angel come down from heaven, clothed with a cloud: and a rainbow [was] upon his head, and his face [was] as it were the sun, and his feet as pillars of fire: {10:2} And he had in his hand a little book open: and he set his right foot upon the sea, and [his] left [foot] on the earth, {10:3} And cried with a loud voice, as [when] a lion roars: and when he had cried, seven thunders uttered their voices. {10:4} and when the seven thunders had uttered their voices, I was about to write: and I heard a voice from heaven saying unto me, seal up those things which the seven thunders uttered, and write them not."

This is the second time John saw a "powerful or strong" angel. As before, this might suggest the loudness and authority of his voice.

(LXXNT-Revelation) "¹And I saw another powerful angel coming down out of heaven, wrapped in a cloud, and a nimbus ("halo or aura") above his head, and his face like the sun, and his legs (The Greek word here is the word for feet, but in ancient Greek and in many languages the words for foot or for hand can mean the whole extremity or whole limb. That is especially true in Revelation, which displays Aramaic influence. It is far more appropriate to speak of a leg being like a column or pillar than a foot being like a pillar) like columns of fire, ² and holding in his hands a little scroll that was opened. And he placed his right foot upon the sea, and his left upon the land, ³ and he cried out with a great voice, like a lion roaring. And when he had cried out, the seven thunders spoke with their sounds (Or, "with their voices."). ⁴ and when the seven thunders had spoken, I was about to write, and I heard a voice from heaven saying, "Seal up what things the seven thunders have spoken, and do not write them." (this was still in the time of the Apostle John and these things were to be sealed until the times of the end, like the book of Daniel) ⁵ And the angel which I had seen standing on the sea and on the land, he lifted his right hand to heaven, ⁶ and swore by Him who lives for ever and ever, who gave birth to the heaven and the things in it, and to the earth and the things in it, and to the sea and the things in it, *he swore* that there shall be no more time, 7 but that in the days of the blast of the seventh angel, whenever he is about to sound his trumpet, even then will be brought to completion the mystery of God, as he has announced it to his servants the prophets. 8 and the voice that I had heard from heaven, it spoke with me again, and said, "Go take the scroll that is opened in the hand of the angel who is standing on the sea and on the land." 9 And I went over to the angel, asking him to give me the little scroll. And he says to me, "Take it and eat it, and it will make your stomach bitter, though in your mouth it will be sweet like honey." 10 And I took the little scroll from the hand of the angel, and I ate it, and in my mouth, it was sweet like honey. And after I had eaten it, my stomach was made bitter. 11 and they are saying to me, "You must again prophesy concerning many peoples and nations and languages and kings."

(MTJ-Revelation) "And I saw another strong malach descending and coming down out of Shomayim, having been wrapped in an anan ("cloud"), and the keshet be'anan ("rainbow", BERESHIS 9:16) was over his rosh ("head") and the face of him was as the shemesh ("sun") and the feet of him as pillars of eish ("fire"), [YECHEZKEL 1:28] |2| And he had in his hand a sefer katan ("small book, small scroll") which had been opened and he placed his ragel hayemanit ("right foot") on the yam ("sea"), and the smolit ("left") on ha'aretz ("the earth"), |3| And he cried with a kol gadol ("loud voice") as an aryeh ("lion") roars. And when he shouted, the shivat hare'amim ("seven thunders") reverberated. [HOSHEA 11:10] |4| And when the shivat hare'amim ("seven thunders") spoke, I was about to write, and I heard a kol ("voice") from Shomayim, saying, Put a chotam ("seal") on [*the sod, the secret of*] what the shivat hare'amim ("seven thunders") have spoken, and seal it up, and do not write, [DANIEL 8:26; 12:4,9] |5| And the malach, whom I saw having taken his stand on the yam (sea) and on ha'aretz ("the earth"), lifted his yamin ("right hand") to Shomayim [DEVARIM 32:40; DANIEL 12:7] |6| And made shevu'ah ("oath") by the One who lives l'Olmei Olamim ("forever and ever or literally Amen Amens") whose "barah" ("created") the Shomayim and the things in it and ha'aretz and the things in it and the yam and the things in it--that there would be no od zman ("more time"). [BERESHIS 14:22; SHEMOT 6:8; BAMIDBAR 14:30; TEHILLIM 115:15; 146:6] |7| But in the days of the sounding of the shofar by the malach hashev'i'i ("the seventh angel"), when he is about to blow the shofar, also then the raz ("mystery") of Hashem would be brought to an end, as he proclaimed to his avadim ("servants"), the Nevi'im ("prophets"). [AMOS 3:7] |8| And the kol ("voice") which I heard from Shomayim was again speaking with me and saying, Go, take the sefer which is opened in the hand of the malach who has taken his stand on the yam ("sea") and on the ha'aretz ("the earth"). |9| And I went to the malach, telling him to give me the sefer katan ("small book") and he says to me, Take and eat it, and it will make your stomach bitter, but in your mouth, it will be sweet as devash ("honey"). [YIRMEYAH 15:16; YECHEZKEL 2:8-3:3] |10| And I took the sefer katan out of the hand of the malach and ate it, and it was in my mouth as sweet as devash ("honey"), but, when I ate, my stomach was made bitter. |11| and they say to me, you must speak dvarim hanevu'ah ("words of prophecy") again, about haumim ("peoples") and Goyim ("Nations") and leshonot ("tongues") and many melachim ("kings"). [Ezekiel 37:4, 9; Daniel 3:4]" John was consigned to write this Revelation to the people of the world.

(LXX-Ezekiel 3) "And he said to me, Son of Man, eat this volume, and go and speak to the children of Israel. So, he opened my mouth, and caused me to eat the volume. And he said to me, Son of man, thy mouth shall eat, and thy belly shall be filled with this volume that is given to thee. So, I ate it; and it was in my mouth as sweet as honey."

The words became bitter because the House of Israel refused to listen to Ezekiel.

Like Daniel, John is not allowed to reveal what is in the small scroll as it is not yet time of the end, but rather eat it. With the sounding of trumpet 7 "there is no more time". The angel "lifted up his right hand" and made an oath. Angels do not make oaths to HaShem. This must be someone of divine nobility, possibly Christ, but who else could it be to declare there is no more time. During the time of Daniel, Christ made such an appearance to the 3 wise men tossed into the furnace of Nebuchadnezzar.

The smoke released from the pit is able to obscure the light of the sun and moon.

- **New Temple:** (KJ-Revelation) "{11:1} and there was given me a reed like unto a rod: and the angel stood, saying, Rise, and measure the temple of God, and the altar, and them that worship therein. {11:2} But the court which is without the temple leave out, and measure it not; for it is given unto the

Gentiles: and the holy city shall they tread under foot forty [and] two months"

This takes place when the two witnesses are taken up and the city of Jerusalem is trod by the gentiles (unbelievers of Christ). This goes along with the Abomination which takes place very shortly during the middle of the Tribulation after Lucifer is cast out of heaven.

(LXX-Ezekiel 43) "Moreover he brought me to the gate looking eastward, and led me forth. And, behold, the glory of the God of Israel came by the eastern way; and *there was* a voice of an army, as the sound of many redoubling *their shouts*, and the earth shone like light from the glory round about... 44:1 then he brought me back by the way of the outer gate of the sanctuary that looks eastward; and it was shut. And the Lord said to me, this gate shall be shut, it shall not be opened, and no one shall pass through it; for the Lord God of Israel shall enter by it, and it shall be shut. For the prince, he shall sit in it, to eat bread before the Lord; he shall go in by the way of the porch of the gate, and shall go forth by the way of the same."

- **Two Witnesses Part 2 (End of 2$^{nd}$ Woe):** (KJ-Revelation) "{11:3} and I will give [power] unto my two witnesses, and they shall prophesy a thousand two hundred [and] threescore days, clothed in sackcloth. {11:4} these are the two olive trees, and the two candlesticks standing before the God of the earth. {11:5} and if any man will hurt them, fire proceeds out of their mouth, and devours their enemies: and if any man will hurt them, he must in this manner be killed. {11:6} these have power to shut heaven that it rains not in the days of their prophecy: and have power over waters to turn them to blood, and to smite the earth with all plagues, as often as they will. {11:7} and when they shall have finished their testimony, the beast ("therion-beast, animal like", STRG2342) that ascended out of the bottomless pit shall make war against them, and shall overcome them, and kill them. {11:8} and their dead bodies [shall lie] in the street of the great city, which spiritually is called Sodom and Egypt, where also our Lord was crucified. {11:9} and they of the people and kindred and tongues and nations shall see their dead bodies three days and a half, and shall not suffer their dead bodies to be put in graves. {11:10} and they that dwell upon the earth shall rejoice over them, and make merry, and shall send gifts one to another; because these two prophets tormented them that dwelt on the earth. {11:11} and after three days and a half the Spirit of life from God entered into them, and they stood upon their feet; and great fear fell upon them which saw them. {11:12} and they heard a great voice from heaven saying unto them, Come up hither. And they ascended up to heaven in a cloud; and their enemies beheld them. {11:13} and the same hour was there a great earthquake, and the tenth part of the city fell, and in the earthquake were slain of men seven thousand: and the remnant were affrighted, and gave glory to the God of heaven. {11:14} the second woe is past; [and,] behold, the third woe cometh quickly."

(LXXNT-Revelation) "³ And I will give *authority* to my two witnesses, and they will prophesy for 1,260 days clothed in sackcloth." ⁴ These are the two olive trees and the two lampstands which stand before the Lord ("theos - supreme deity", STRG2316) of the earth (Zechariah 4:3, 14 these two lampstands are Elijah and Enoch, the two human beings who never died. Their flames never went out; they are witnesses who have never slept in the grave, eyes that have never closed.). ⁵ and if anyone wants to harm them, fire comes from their mouth and consumes their enemies. And if anyone would want to harm them, this is how he ought to be killed. ⁶ These have the authority to shut up the sky so that no rain will fall during the days of their prophesying, and they have authority over the waters to turn them into blood, and to strike the earth with any kind of plague as often as they wish. ⁷ and when they complete their witness, the beast ("therion - beast, wild beast", STRG2342) coming up out of the bottomless pit will make war with them, and will conquer them and kill them. ⁸ and their corpses *lie* on the boulevard of the great city which is spiritually named Sodom and Egypt, where also their Lord was crucified. ⁹ and from peoples and tribes and languages and nations they see their corpses for three and a half days. And they are not allowing their corpses to be placed in a grave. ¹⁰ and those dwelling on the earth rejoice (The Textus Receptus has the future indicative rather than the present indicative of rejoice, and the Byzantine has the present. Yet, the Byzantine has the future indicative for the next verb, celebrate, but the present for "they see" in verse 9) over them, and celebrate, and will send gifts ("they will send") to one another. For these two prophets had tormented those dwelling on the earth. ¹¹ and after three and a half days, the breath of life from God went into them, and they stood up on their feet. And great fear fell over those watching them. ¹² and they heard a great voice from heaven saying to them, "Come up here." And they went up into heaven in a cloud, and their enemies watched them. ¹³and in that hour ("hora- hour, instant", STRG5610) a great earthquake took place, and one tenth of the city collapsed, and 7,000 people were killed. And the survivors were terrified, and they gave glory to the God of heaven."

They were dead for 3 and a half days, the same number of days that Christ was in the grave at the crucifixion. The two added together comes to 7 days, the total number of days of the Creation. His Torah requires two witnesses (Deuteronomy 19: 15, 17: 6) and Y'shua confirmed this in Joh 8: 17. Again we see that even in the future Tribulation Period the Torah will be upheld. There is also a strong possibility that Daniel 12: 5-10 also refers to these two witnesses. There are various theories concerning the timing of the two witnesses.

It is possible that the earthquake of the two witnesses is the same earthquake of either seal 6 or beginning of seal 7.

(LXX-Malachi 4) "And, behold, I will send to you Elias the Thesbite, before the great and glorious day of the Lord comes".

This could refer to John the Baptist but also to one of the two witnesses.

(LXX-Daniel 12) "And thou, Daniel, close the words, and seal the book to the time of the end; until many are taught, and knowledge is increased. And I Daniel saw, and, behold, two others stood, on one side of the bank of the river, and the other on the other side of the bank of the river"

(MTJ-Revelation) "|3| And I will give to my Sh'ney HaEdim ("Two Witnesses") and they will speak divrei haNevu'ah ("words of prophecy") one thousand two hundred and sixty days (this is 3 and 1 half year if the year is 360 days long) having been clothed in sakkim ("sackcloth"). [BERESHIS 37:34; SHMUEL BAIS 3:31; NECHEMYAH 9:1] |4| these are the two olive trees and the two menorot standing before the Adon kol ha'aretz. [TEHILLIM 52:8; YIRMEYAH 11:16; ZECHARYAH 4:3, 11, 14] |5| and if anyone wants to harm them, eish ("fire") comes out of their mouth and destroys their oyevim ("enemies"); and if anyone wants to harm them, it is necessary for him to be killed like this. [SHMUEL BAIS 22:9; MELACHIM BAIS 1:10; YIRMEYAH 5:14; BAMIDBAR 16:29, 35] |6|

these have the samchut ("authority") to shut Shomayim that no geshem ("rain") may fall during the days of their nevu'ah ("prophecy"). And samchut ("authority") they have over the waters to turn them into dahm and to strike ha'aretz with makkot ("plagues") of every kind, as often as they want. [SHEMOT 7:17, 19 [MELACHIM ALEF 17:1] |7| and when they complete the edut ("testimony") of them, the Chayyah ("Beast, Anti- Moshiach") coming up from the Tehom ("Abyss") will make war with them and will conquer them and will kill them. [DANIEL 7:21] |8| And the NEVELAH ("corpse", DEVARIM 21:23) of them will be on the rekhov ("street") of the Ir Hagadol, which, spiritually, is called S'dom and Mitzrayim ("Egypt"), where also the Adon of them was pierced on the etz. [YESHAYAH 1:9; YIRMEYAH 13:14; YECHEZKEL 16:46] |9| And some of haummim (the peoples) and shevatim ("tribes") and leshonot ("languages") and Goyim ("Nations") see the NEVELAH of them for shloshah and a half yamim and the NEVELAH of them they do not permit to be put into a kever ("tomb"). [TEHILLIM 79:2, 3] |10| and the ones dwelling on ha'aretz ("the earth") rejoice with great simcha ("joy") over them and make merry and they will send matanot ("gifts") to one another, because these two nevi'im ("prophets") tormented the ones dwelling on ha'aretz ("the earth"). [Nehemiah 8:10, 12; Esther 9:19, 22] |11| and after the shloshah ("three") and a half yamim ("days"), a Ruach of Chayyim from Hashem entered into them, and they stood up upon their feet, and pachad Gadol ("great terror") fell upon the ones seeing them. [YECHEZKEL 37:5, 9, 10, 14] |12| and they heard a kol gadol ("loud voice") out of Shomayim saying to them, "Come up here!" And they went up into Shomayim in the anan ("cloud"), and their oyevim ("enemies") saw them. [MELACHIM BAIS 2:11] |13| and in that hour occurred a great earthquake and the tenth part of the city fell and there were killed in the earthquake shivat alafim ("seven thousand"), and the rest became afraid and gave kavod ("glory") to Elohei HaShomayim."

(LXX-Ezekiel 3) "Then the Spirit took me up, and I heard behind me the voice *as* of a great earthquake, *saying*, blessed *be* the glory of the Lord from his place." Ezekiel predicted the earthquake following the eating of the little scroll.

This event takes place at the end of the first 3 and a half years of the tribulation. By the Yovel interpretation, this does not present a problem, as they first appear at the beginning of seal 7. Many will believe these 2 to be evil because of the destruction they bring. The witnesses will resume preaching the *Gospel of the*

*Kingdom* which was started by John the Baptist. For the next 7 years, the Anti-Christ will blaspheme the Holy One. These 2 witnesses are the 2 olive trees and the 2 lampstands that stand before HaShem. They will call a famine for the entire term of their witness and they have power to turn water to blood (the first plague from the time of the Exodus) and to strike the earth with every plague. The beast was released during trumpet 5 by the fallen angel opening the pit.

These plagues are in addition to the plagues of the seals. The opening of the 6 seals takes place before the 2 witnesses, giving more support for a 50-year period of the seals, where the first 6 seals are opened in years 1 – 42 of the Yovel cycle and are not part of the Tribulation Week.

For those who interpret the seals all being opened in 1 week of 7 years, the 2 witnesses are alive during the opening of all 7 seals. The trumpets are opened in the first half of the Tribulation as well as they come before Satan is cast out and before the 2 witnesses are taken to heaven.

"And when they complete their witness, the beast ("therion – beast, wild beast", STRG2342) coming up out of the bottomless pit will make war with them, and will conquer them and kill them." This says that at the *end* of their testimony the beast will come out of the bottomless pit (at the middle of the week of tribulation). This is often interpreted to be the Anti-Christ, but the Anti-Christ is believed to attain his kingdom at the beginning of the tribulation and at the beginning of the testimony of the two witnesses, possibly even sooner, as he must rule over the 10 kingdoms or 10 toes of the image of Nebuchadnezzar. This beast didn't exist on earth until a fallen angel opened the pit. Daniel says that the Anti-Christ will make a covenant with Israel for 1 week of years. With the 1-week interpretation, this covenant takes place during the opening of the seals. With the Yovel interpretation, this covenant starts with the opening of seal 7 and does not present any problem. Halfway through the tribulation, the covenant is broken. This will take place when Satan is cast out of heaven and commits the abomination of desolation in the Temple.

It is not known for certain if "in that hour" or "in that instant" is literal or figurative, but it is likely that in this case the words are literally meant to be in that hour of time. The earthquake is the third earthquake of this huge nature (the first being between seal 5 and 6 and the second being at the beginning of seal 7). The mark of HaShem over His believers protects believers from most of the events of the seals, but they will not be protected from the earthquake here that kills 7000 people. The remaining believers "give glory to Hashem".

Both Judas and the Anti-Christ are called the Devil (John 6:70-71). He wasn't *just demon possessed.* He was the Devil incarnate. The Beast shall come from the same Abyss where Judas was sent after his death, but the words for Beast and Anti-Christ are different meaning this beast does not appear to be humanlike.

This marks the end of the halfway mark of the 7-year tribulation (no matter which interpretation you accept). They started at the beginning of the tribulation week and this is now 3 and 1 half years into the tribulation.

By Theory 1 (7-year theory that the seals are all opened in a 7-year period), 7 of the seals were opened and 6 trumpets blown in the first 3 and a half years. By Theory 2 (50 year opening of the seals), all 7 seals have been opened during a 46-year period.

The date is 5995.06 AT by MT

7419.06 AT by LXX

2932 CE by Julian calendar

**Trumpet 7:** (KJ-Revelation) "{11:13} *and the same hour* was there a great earthquake, and the tenth part of the city fell, and in the earthquake were slain of men seven thousand: and the remnant (of believers) were affrighted, and gave glory to the God of heaven. {11:14} the second woe is past; [and,] behold, the third woe cometh quickly. {11:15} and the seventh angel sounded; and there were great voices in heaven, saying, the kingdoms of this world are become [the kingdoms] of our Lord, and of his Christ; and he shall reign for ever and ever. {11:16} and the four and twenty elders, which sat before God on their seats, fell upon their faces, and worshipped God, {11:17} Saying, we give thee thanks, O Lord God Almighty, which art, and was, and art to come; because thou hast taken to thee thy great power, and hast reigned. {11:18} and the nations were angry, and thy wrath is come, and the time of the dead, that they should be judged, and that thou should give reward unto thy servants the prophets, and to the saints, and them that fear thy name, small and great; and should destroy them which destroy the earth."

This clarifies that the earthquake of the 2 witnesses is the same earthquake of trumpet 7.

The remnant refers to the remnant of Judah and Israel that believed on Him but this is no longer limited to Israel, but the remnant of "all believers". This confirms that the resurrection called the Rapture has not yet taken place.

(KJ-Daniel 7) "{7:7} after this I saw in the night visions, and behold a fourth beast, dreadful and terrible, and strong exceedingly; and it had great iron teeth: it devoured and brake in pieces, and stamped the residue with the feet of it: and it [was] diverse from all the beasts that [were] before it; and it had ten horns. {7:8} I considered the horns, and, behold, there came up among them another little horn, before whom there were three of the first horns plucked up by the roots: and, behold, in this horn [were] eyes like the eyes of man, and a mouth speaking great things {7:9} I beheld till the thrones were cast down, and the Ancient of days did sit, whose garment [was] white as snow, and the hair of his head like the pure wool: his throne [was like] the fiery flame, [and] his wheels [as] burning fire. {7:10} a fiery stream issued and came forth from before him: thousand thousand ministered unto him, and ten thousand times ten thousand stood before him: the judgment was set, and the books were opened. {7:11} I beheld then because of the voice of the great words which the horn spoke: *I beheld [even] till the beast was slain, and his body destroyed, and given to the burning flame. {7:12} as concerning the rest of the beasts, they had their dominion taken away: yet their lives were prolonged for a season and time.* {7:13} I saw in the night visions, and, behold, [one] like the Son of man came with the clouds of heaven, and came to the Ancient of days, and they brought him near before him. {7:14} and there was given him dominion, and glory, and a kingdom, that all people, nations, and languages, should serve him: his dominion [is] an everlasting dominion, which shall not pass away, and his kingdom [that] which shall not be destroyed."

The 2 witnesses, but at this point in time, they have just died and been risen up. This is the middle of the Tribulation week, no matter which interpretation is believed to be true. "In that hour" that they were taken up a third earthquake struck the earth. This earthquake will strike Jerusalem. The quake will kill 7000 people.

(LXXNT-Revelation) "¹⁵ and the seventh angel sounded his trumpet; and there were great voices in heaven, saying, "The kingdom(s) of the world has become the kingdom of our Lord, and of his Christ! (His anointed) And he shall reign for ever and ever!" ¹⁶ and the twenty-four elders, who sit on their thrones before God, ("before the throne of God") fell on their faces and worshiped God, ¹⁷ saying, "We thank you, Lord God Almighty, who is and who was ("and who is to come, because") that you have taken that great power of yours and begun to reign. ¹⁸ and the nations have become angry, and your anger also has come, and the time for the dead to be judged, and reward to be given to your servants the prophets and to the saints and to those fearing your name, both small and great, and to destroy the ones destroying the earth. ¹⁹ and the temple of God in heaven opened, and the ark of his covenant was seen in his temple; and there came peals of thunder, and noises and rumblings and an earthquake ("seismos-earthquake, commotion", STRG4578) (fourth earthquake since seal 6 opened, The Philoxenian Syriac has "fire" instead of earthquake), and large hailstones."Fire is in line with volcanoes shooting hailstones of fire and the volcanic explosions would cause earthquakes.

(LXXTR-Revelation) "15 And the seventh angel sounded his trumpet; and there were great voices in heaven, saying, "The kingdoms of the world have become the kingdom of our Lord, and of his Christ! (His anointed) And he shall reign for ever and ever!" 16 And the twenty-four elders, who sit on their thrones before God, fell on their faces and worshiped God, 17 saying, "We thank you, Lord God Almighty, who is and who was, that you have taken that great power of yours and begun to reign. 18 And the nations have become angry, and your anger also has come, and the time for the dead to be judged, and reward to be given to your servants the prophets and to the saints and to those fearing your name, both small and great, and to destroy the ones destroying the earth." 19 And the temple of God in heaven opened, and the ark of his covenant was seen in his temple; and there came peals of thunder, and noises and rumblings and an earthquake, and large hailstones."

(MTJ-Revelation) "|15| and the malach hashevi'i ("the seventh angel") sounded his shofar. And there were kolot gedolim ("loud voices") in Shomayim, saying, "The Malchut of the Olam Hazeh became the Malchut of Adoneinu and of His Moshiach, and He will reign l'Olemei Olamim. [Psalms 145:13; Daniel 2:44; 7:14, 27; Micah 4:7; Zechariah 14:9] |16| and the esrim v'arba'ah Zekenim ("twenty-four Elders", SHEMOT 12:21), sitting on their kisot before Hashem, fell on their faces and worshiped Hashem, |17| Saying, "Modim Anachnu ("We give thanks"), Adonoi Elokeinu, El Shaddai ("God almighty"), the One who is and the One who was, because you have taken your oz gadol ("great power") and reigned. [TEHILLIM 30:12] |18| And the Goyim ("Nations") raged. And your Charon af ("burning wrath") came, and the zman ("time") for the Mesim to be judged and for giving the sachar ("reward") to your avadim ("servants"), the nevi'im ("prophets") and the Kadoshim and the ones fearing ha-Shem of you, the ketanim ("small") and the gedolim ("great"), and for destroying the ones destroying ha'aretz (the earth). [TEHILLIM 2:1] |19| And the Heikhal ("Temple") of Hashem was opened in Shomayim, and the Aron HaBrit ("Ark of the Covenant") of Hashem was seen in the Heikhal of Hashem. And there were flashes of lightning and kolot ("sounds") and thunders and an earthquake and great barad ("hail"). [Exodus25:10 22; 2 Chronicles 5:7]"

It does not say where the hailstones come from. There are 2 very good possibilities; 1 from a passing comet that comes close to earth much like the comet Typhon did at the time of the Exodus, and 2 from active volcanoes firing off as in the days of Pompeii. The volcano shot hail of stone and fire for thousands of miles. A few volcanoes going off with the earthquakes would be considered a valid possibility.

This takes place *after* the resurrection of the 2 witnesses or at the same time, meaning that this event takes place soon after the middle of the Tribulation Week. In the 1 week of year's interpretation, this is after all the seals of the scroll have been opened 3 and a half years in unless in that interpretation, it is believed that this goes back in time to the middle of the week.

In the Yovel of year's interpretation, this is during the opening of seal 7 in the last week of Yovel cycle 120. Six weeks of years (42 years) have passed since the opening of the first seal.

All the seals have been opened (by both interpretations) and the trumpets and vials have given their plagues. *Christ has been given dominion over all the nations.* Satan is cast down out of heaven and the two witnesses have been taken to heaven and it says here that NOW, Christ begins his rule. The beast was slain but the 10 nations continued for a "season and a time". We know from Daniel that a time is about a year. A season is part of a year. But from this we know that at THIS time in the Revelation of John, the Tribulation is over. Christ becomes King is reported just before Satan is cast out of heaven and the war with the angels of Satan against the angels of Michael.

- **Temple of God is opened in heaven:** (KJ-Revelation) "{11:19} and the temple of God was opened in heaven, and there was seen in his temple the ark of his testament: and there were lightnings, and voices, and thunderings, and an earthquake, and great hail."
- **Trumpet Relationship to the Crucifixion of Christ:** When Christ hung on the cross, all 4 of the results of the trumpets was revealed in the Cross:

k. Trumpet 1: Tree = Cross

l. Trumpet 2: Blood = Blood of Christ spilled from the many wounds from the thrashing He took.

m. Trumpet 3: Gall = He was given bitter vinegar or gall to drink.

n. Trumpet 4: Sun went dark = Sun went dark for several hours while He hung on the Cross.

o. The three woes indicate His death on the cross.

p. Trumpet 5: He went into the pit. He conquered death, but here in this trumpet, men would seek death and not find it. The locusts had breastplates of iron, a metal related to the Roman Empire, and it was by Roman soldiers that Christ hung on the Cross. Christ rose from the pit, having the key to death. One woe is past that is the death of Christ in the grave. Two woes remain.

q. Trumpet 6: Christ went to be with the father and His voice will come from the altar where He resides until "His Time to return again".

r. The little scroll and 7 thunders represent the 7 churches through the Church Period.

s. Trumpet 7: Kingdoms have become 1 and Christ takes His throne to rule for 1000 years.

t. The trumpet calls here (7th trumpet) is related to the trumpet calls of Joshua when he defeated Jericho.

# Chapter 16

## Summary

There are many Christians who believe that going to church once or twice a week and giving the Bible a cursory read once in a while and claiming that they "believe in God" is enough to get them to heaven, their goal. Just... get to heaven. This has become the mainstream of a great majority of Christians.

Preachers like to take count of "those who repeat the sinner's prayer" and how much money they can collect. After that, if the person shows up and gives the church their duly deserved tithe, well, that person must be okay. They shake hands at the door after the service... "Thank you Mr... or Mrs. Blah blah... Going to watch the game today?" That person's personal state in the true Church of God is never challenged or questioned by the preachers as long as that person shows up and gives them money.

Service, "true" service to the Living God is "hard" and yet, so so easy. You don't even have to follow the Laws of Moses. Just live by one rule: "...by every word from the mouth of God".

If God says to do something, do it

If God says not to do something, don't do it.

If God says nothing, He's leaving the choice up to you, but this only accounts for a very small percentage of choices in life.

HaShem is actively seeking to be a big part of your life.

This service will be challenged by those who are "close to you". "Did God really say?" The words of the Serpent ring forth from the Garden not just to Eve but to everyone who tries to live a devoted life to God.

If you live your day to day life without consulting that still small voice inside, then you are missing out on a HUGE relationship that is viewed by many to be "Just too much work and you have to do all this stuff that doesn't allow time for TV, for sports, for hobbies..." and that's true. It will cause your life to be limited from "having fun", "enjoying life", "taking it easy", and "Just plain relaxing".

A call to service by HaShem is a life changing experience. I can recall listening to a service in the basement of a Presbyterian Church by a speaker who started his sermon by turning his message over to God for God to use his mouth. As I listened to the man, I suddenly felt terrified. So terrified that I slid off my metal folding chair to my knees.

Some reading this will say...See? That must have been a false voice, a demon or something. NO... Read the Bible again and see how many times when God spoke to people, Abraham, Moses, etc. and they felt "terror". Because coming into direct contact with the living God is a terrifying experience. His presence will confront your sinful nature that we inherited from Adam and Eve. Your empty life will be forced into your own review and everything you thought was important will be reduced to in that moment to emptiness.

Once you have heard the voice of God, there is nothing like it. I've been to hundreds of churches and listened to many more preachers and never have I heard anyone speak the way that man spoke that night. I have searched for someone, anyone to speak with the voice of God instead of their own ego giving a cute sermon with added jokes for entertainment.

But.... Until HaShem "calls YOU" there's nothing you can do. You can't make God call you to service. And if He does, it doesn't mean that you're going to be some great warrior for God, a prophet, an evangelist. God calls the lowly. Read the prophets and see how many were great before God called them. Amos was a simple sheepherder.

I'm not famous. I'm not rich. I've never reached the status of being a "smashing success". I'm just a simple man who answered God's call and I wouldn't trade this life for all the gold in Fort Knox.

# Chapter 17

## Abbreviations

Date and Bible versions are repeated numerous times so it is expedient to use abbreviations that are used often:

A.Abr   Year from birth of Abraham

A.Ad   Anno Adam or Year from Adam's creation (which is really redundant as this is the same as the Date from creation AT or AM).

AD (also C.E.) Anno Domini (Year from the Crucifixion or Current Era - 1 A.D. to 6000 A.D)

AKL   Aryan King List of India (also known as Puranas)

AM   Anno Mundi (Year of the World - used by Hebrews for their dates).

A.U.M.6Year of Rome (from foundation of Rome in 753 BC)

AT Anno Torah (Year of the Bible from Creation).

MAT A.T.       date based on Masoretic Text

LAT A.T.       date based on LXX

SAT A.T.       date based on Samaritan Text

LVAT A.T.      date based on Latin Vulgate

BC    Before Current Era or Before Christ

BDB   Brown's Drivers and Briggs (Hebrew word reference)

BLXX   Holy Bible, Berean Greek Bible, BGB Copyright ©2016 by Bible Hub Used by Permission. All Rights Reserved Worldwide

BOE    Book of Enoch translated by Robert Bagley III in 2016

BOJ    Book of Jasher Faithfully translated (1840) from the Original Hebrew into English.

BOJU   Book of Jubilee

CE     Current Era (used interchangeably with AD)

D      Abr. Year from Death of Abraham

DT     Dies Torah (Day count from day 1 of Creation)

HC     Hebrew Chronology

IKL    Isin King List

JA     Julius Africanus

JC     Julian calendar

JD     Julian Day Count (from November 4713 BC)

JOS    Josephus, Flavius. The Works of Flavius Josephus

JPS    Jewish Publication Society King James Version 1917

JPS2   Jewish Publication Society of 1962

JUBA   Book of Jubilees from Adam based on 50-year Jubilee)

JUBD   Jubilees from David (50-year Jubilee)

KJ     King James from 1611 Version

LAB    Liber antiquitatum biblicarum

LD     Lilian Day Count (from Oct 11, 1582 C.E. when Gregorian calendar became official)

LV     Latin Vulgate

LXX     Septuagint Bible SIR LANCELOT C.L. BRENTON: Originally published by Samuel Bagster & Sons, Ltd., London 1851

LXXNT New Testament Translation by Robert Palmer December 08 2022 Edition.

LXXRP May 28, 2023 translation by David Robert Palmer.

LXXTR Septuagint Textus Receptus Edition April 10, 2023 edition by David Robert Palmer

MT      Masoretic Text Jewish Publication Society 1917

MTJ     Masoretic Orthodox Jewish Text of the Bible

PB      Parshas Bereshis (Book of Genesis only)

RD      Rata Dies Day Count (From Jan 1, 1 C.E. – First day after B.C.E. period of history)

SKL     Sumerian King List

SO,     Seder Olam (Hebrew Chronology from 169 A.D.

SQ      Status Quo or Conventional History

ST      Samaritan Text (Pentateuch Only)

STRH    Strong's Hebrew

STRG    Strong's Greek

TO      Targum Onkelos: The First Five Books of the Bible

WLC     Westminster Leningrad Codex 1917 by Jewish Publication Society.

WY      Wycliffe Bib

www.ingramcontent.com/pod-product-compliance
Lightning Source LLC
LaVergne TN
LVHW021829060526
838201LV00058B/3574